500 TILES

D1225727

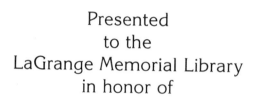

Presented
to the
LaGrange Memorial Library
in honor of

Dr. William B. Fackler Jr.
2008

500 TILES

AN INSPIRING COLLECTION OF INTERNATIONAL WORK

LARK
BOOKS

A Division of
Sterling Publishing Co., Inc.
New York / London

SENIOR EDITOR
Suzanne J. E. Tourtillott

ART DIRECTOR
Matt Shay, Shay Design

COVER DESIGNER
Cindy LaBreacht

FRONT COVER
Tim Ludwig
Agen Tulip, 2006
Photo by Randy Smith

BACK COVER
Brian J. Boldon
Amy Baur
View from a Distance, Corner Mural, 2006
Photos by Amy Baur / In Plain Sight

SPINE
Jeff Reich
Agave, 2006
Photo by Farraday Newsome

FRONT FLAP
(TOP):
Meredith MacLeod
Nuthatch, 2006
Photo by artist

(BOTTOM):
Michael C. Hoffman
Sting-Ray Freedom Bike #1, 2006
Photo by artist

BACK FLAP
Maggie Mae Beyeler
Ca'd'oro, 2007
Photo by Margot Geist

PAGE 3
Tom O'Malley
Green Mountain Vista II, 2006
Photo by artist

PAGE 5
Susan Wink
Creative Learning Center Mosaic Mural, 2005
Photo by Nancy Fleming

Library of Congress Cataloging-in-Publication Data

Tourtillott, Suzanne J. E.
  500 tiles : an inspiring collection of international work / Suzanne Tourtillott.
    p. cm.
  Includes index.
  ISBN-13: 978-1-57990-714-3 (pb-trade pbk. : alk. paper)
  ISBN-10: 1-57990-714-8 (pb-trade pbk. : alk. paper)
  1. Tiles--Catalogs. 2. Decorative arts--Catalogs. I. Title. II. Title: Five hundred tiles.
  NK4670.T68 2008
  738.6--dc22
                                        2007028980

10 9 8 7 6 5 4 3 2 1

First Edition

Published by Lark Books, A Division of
Sterling Publishing Co., Inc.
387 Park Avenue South, New York, N.Y. 10016

Text © 2008, Lark Books
Photography © 2007, Artist/Photographer

Distributed in Canada by Sterling Publishing,
c/o Canadian Manda Group, 165 Dufferin Street
Toronto, Ontario, Canada M6K 3H6

Distributed in the United Kingdom by GMC Distribution Services,
Castle Place, 166 High Street, Lewes, East Sussex, England BN7 1XU

Distributed in Australia by Capricorn Link (Australia) Pty Ltd.,
P.O. Box 704, Windsor, NSW 2756 Australia

If you have questions or comments about this book, please contact:
Lark Books
67 Broadway
Asheville, NC 28801
828-253-0467

Manufactured in China

ISBN 13: 978-1-57990-714-3
ISBN 10: 1-57990-714-8

For information about custom editions, special sales, premium and corporate purchases, please contact Sterling Special Sales Department at 800-805-5489 or specialsales@sterlingpub.com.

Contents

Introduction

Given the mission of assembling such a formidable collection, it would stand to reason that I should first set out to define its context. Referring to Merriam-Webster's, I find *tile: a flat or curved piece of fired clay, stone, or concrete used especially for roofs, floors, or walls and often for ornamental work.* While this is a basic and accurate definition, it doesn't even begin to give a sense of what you'll find within the pages of *500 Tiles*. Figuratively as well as literally, both conceptually and technically, the amazing tile work that follows hails from all over the map. Perhaps it is because the "tile," by definition, has such minimal requirements that artists have had the freedom to take this basic element in so many different directions, and why so many artists have been attracted to making tile in the first place. I'm convinced that the tile truly must be the perfect universal vehicle for artistic expression in clay. The possibilities are so broad, so varied and diverse, that I believe tile offers opportunities for every possible interest or inclination, whether it leans towards drawing and painting, photography and printmaking, sculpture, architecture, or even traditional ceramic processes. For all those artists, handmade tile is the canvas, whose primary function is to be decorative. So whether as an exquisite individual gem, like Michael Cohen's *Tree*, or as cladding for an entire side of a building, as with Skuja Braden's *Flowers*, the tiles included in this book were principally designed for visual appreciation.

Through tile, many ceramists have been able to relax some of their concerns with form and instead are able to concentrate primarily on surface treatment, utilizing textural clay, glazes, and atmospheric firings as their brushes. These ceramic "brushes" are illustrated on the wonderful tile "canvases" of Georgette Zirbes's *Timeline Triptych #1*, Elizabeth A. Vorlicek's *Finger Printed Tile Box*, and Tony Moore's *Botanicals and Cross*, respectively. In yet another instance of ceramists bringing a pottery vernacular to the tile table, Rosalind Redfern creates her tiles by throwing them on the wheel as in *Copper Red Tile Panel*.

Ceramic tile offers two-dimensional artists a richer—not to mention more durable—surface to draw and paint on than do paper or canvas. The ability to sgraffito through wetware slip and majolica glazes and the translucency and color intensity of glazes add depth that can never be attained with conventional drawing mediums. Just as in the two-dimensional art world, there are many different painting and drawing styles and techniques. There's the playful and naive style of Frank Ozereko's *Horse*; the sharp, crisp pen and ink lines of Bob Pike's *Truck* drawings; the Matisse-like quality of Karen S. Kraemer's *Crazy Room*; and, if it were on a larger scale, Greg Daly's *Decorated Tile with Gold/Silver Leaf and Enamel* could easily hold its own next to any outsize, abstract, color-field painting.

While all the tiles in this book could be considered as essentially decorative in nature, they are not by any means vacuous. There are several artists, like Jenny Mendes and Valerie Nicklow, whose tile images present us with a very personal, bizarre, and mysterious narrative. Richard Notkin's work makes political commentary, while Doug Spalding's *Obey* and Rick Nickel's *Cars Men Drive* offer whimsy and humor.

You'll find that a great majority of the tiles utilize relief in some form or other. Linda Kliewer's *Maple Leaves* relief is delicate and shallow, barely pushing off the picture plane, while Susan Beiner's reliefs seem to practically explode out of the tile's surface, as if threatening to invade our physical world. Some artists' approach to relief sculpting is smooth and stylized, as with *Two Blackbirds in Reeds* by Laura McCaul, while others utilize a more direct, roughly or casually hewn technique, as do Merla Frazey-Jordan and Ron Mazanowski's *Alpine Locoweed*. Working within the condensed sculptural plane of relief, it's fun and tempting to play with exaggerated perspectives, as you can see with the work of Ian F. Thomas's *Now and Later*, Rebeca D. Gilling's *Rosemary*, and *Cake & Friend* by Judith Berk King.

Speaking of dimension, a few artists went beyond tile as sculptural relief and moved it into the realm of sculpture itself. Tom O'Malley's *Green Mountain Vista 1* and Sara Behling's *Healing Wound* tile pieces have the presence of sculptural objects while still retaining the elements that allow them to read as tiles.

While you'll see more artists starting to use tiles in temporary gallery installations, tiles remain a permanent installation workhorse, for when properly installed they can last forever with minimal maintenance requirements. That makes tile one of the favorite mediums for public art commissions,

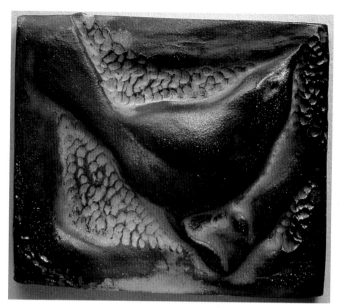

Keri Huber
Catbird | 2005

such as Catharine Magel's ambitious *Reflecting on a River*. Because the tile is an individual unit, it's also a natural for engaging public participation in community art mural projects as Ruth O'Day did with *Leaf Forms*, involving the residents of a neighboring apartment complex in creating elements for the wall mural.

Some new technology is also represented in *500 Tiles*: Brian J. Boldon's *View From a Distance, Corner Mural* utilizes photo-quality images, printed in sublimation ink dyes, for his mural. The results are quite spectacular.

No collection of tile would be complete without some mosaic work. Stephen Bird's Entrance to *Agacan Restaurant*, a delightfully whimsical storefront installation, is a fine example of *piqué assiette* technique. Meanwhile, Shawn Newton's *Lady with Flower* utilizes clay *tesserae* in a more traditional approach to constructing her lovely images. Finally, Rose G. Quintana's little vignettes are another story all together as she employs a range of tile and mosaic techniques.

There is so much more I could say about the wonderful entries contained in this volume, but I think it's time to let you take a look for yourself. The opportunity to view all this amazing tile work has been truly an inspiring delight. Choosing only 500 of them, on the other hand, was a difficult challenge, but I do think this book offers a satisfying sampling of what's being done in the world of art tile today. I want to thank all those artists who so generously submitted their work. Congratulations and good luck on all your future tile adventures. Tile on, and prosper!

—Angelica Pozo

Ann M. Tubbs

Cherries Tile | 2006

4 X 4 X ½ INCHES (10.2 X 10.2 X 1.3 CM)

Slab-rolled and handmade clay; glaze, hand-finished;
maiolica glaze, decorated, electric fired, cone 2

PHOTO BY ARTIST

Brian J. Boldon
Amy Baur

View from a Distance, Corner Mural | 2006

56 X 82 X ½ INCHES (142.2 X 208.3 X 1.3 CM)

Earthenware; white glaze; laser-printed overglaze enamel images; oxidation fired, cone 012; handmade kiln-formed glass tiles; full fused, 1450°F (788°C)

PHOTOS BY AMY BAUR / IN PLAIN SIGHT

Connie Pike
Rooster | 2003
8 X 8 INCHES (20.3 X 20.3 CM)
Buff stoneware; gas fired, cone 10;
overglaze decoration
PHOTO BY ARTIST

Amourentina Louisa Leibman
Icon | 2005

8¹/₂ X 8¹/₂ X ¹/₄ INCHES (21.6 X 21.6 X 0.6 CM)

Earthenware; electric fired; stains on bisque;
transparent glaze over stains, cone 06

PHOTO BY ARTIST

Cristina Delago

Inspired by Hundertwasse | 2006

EACH: 5 X 5 INCHES (12.7 X 12.7 CM)

Low-fired press-molded terra cotta;
electric fired, cone 06; glazed, cone
04; applied glass mosaic

PHOTO BY TOMASZ MAJCHERCZYK

David Crane

Ptolomey Time | 2006

DIAMETER: 30¹¹/₁₆ X 30¹¹/₁₆ INCHES (78 X 78 CM)

Slumped stoneware; slips and engobes; electric fired, cone 6

PHOTOS BY LINDA MURPHY

Wesley L. Smith

Childhood Toys | 2006

14 X 14 X 2 INCHES (35.6 X 35.6 X 5.1 CM)

Stoneware; celadon glaze, reduction fired, cone 10; china paint,
cone 017; platinum and mother-of-pearl lusters, cone 018

PHOTO BY ARTIST

Hennie Meyer
The Swing | 2006
2³/₄ X 2³/₄ X 2³/₄ INCHES (7 X 7 X 7 CM)
Slab-built earthenware, painted slip;
glaze, oxides; electric fired, cone 2
PHOTO BY ARTIST

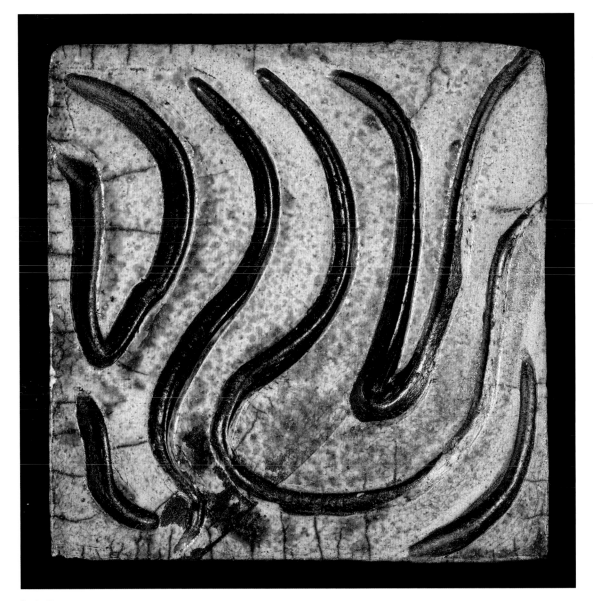

Lai Gong
Blue Energy | 2006
4 X 4 X ½ INCHES (10.2 X 10.2 X 1.3 CM)
Raku clay; copper blue glaze
PHOTO BY TOM CLARK

Paul A. McCoy
Riverbed Series #4 | 2003
11 ½ X 11 ½ X 1 ¾ INCHES (29.2 X 29.2 X 4.4 CM)
Ram-pressed, altered stoneware with deflocculated
slips; gas fired, reduction fired, cone 6
PHOTO BY BOB SMITH

Sandre Griffin

A Bird Out of Hand | 2006

5 5/8 X 5 5/8 X 3/8 INCHES (14.3 X 14.3 X 1 CM)

Slab-rolled white porcelain; black slip and
clear glaze; sgraffito; electric fired, cone 6

PHOTO BY BRYAN JOHNSON

Mary Kuilema
Maple Canopy, Table Top | 2006
14¹/₂ X 28¹/₂ X ¹/₂ INCHES (36.8 X 72.4 X 1.3 CM)
Stoneware; glazed, electric kiln, cone 6
PHOTO BY ARTIST

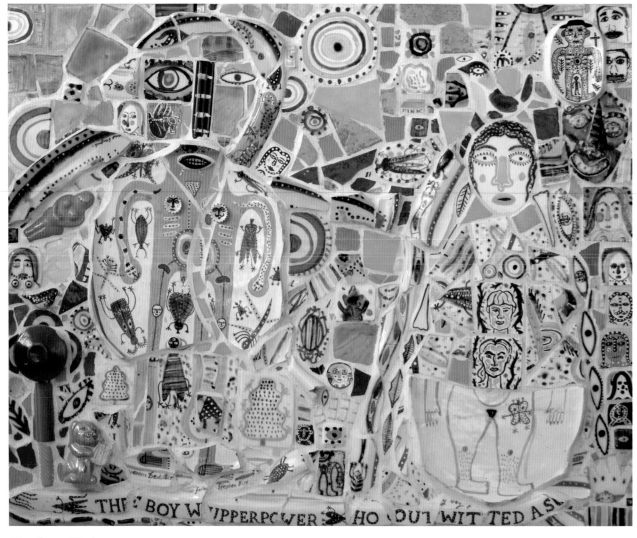

Stephen Bird

The Boy Wupperpower | 2004

31 ¹/₂ X 39³/₈ INCHES (80 X 100 CM)

Wood, cement, earthenware; electric fired; glazed, cone 1

PHOTOS BY ARTIST

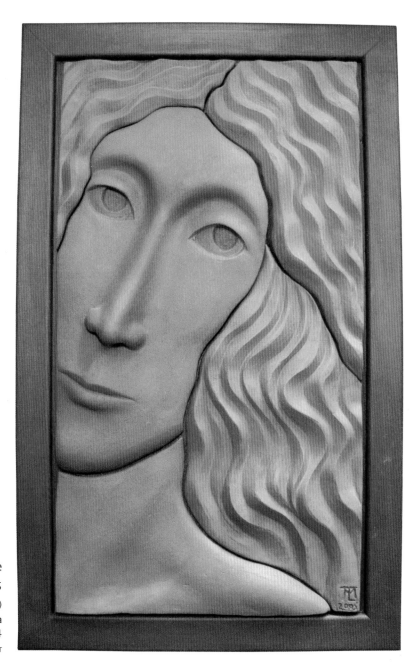

Tracie L. Maryne
Kimberly | 2005
17 1/2 X 10 X 1 INCHES (44.5 X 25.4 X 2.5 CM)
Hand-built, low-fire terra
cotta; electric fired, cone 04
PHOTO BY ARTIST

Lynn Smiser Bowers

Pear Tile | 2007

4 X 4 X ¼ INCHES (10.2 X 10.2 X 0.6 CM)

Hand-cut porcelain slab; wax resist, oxides, stencils; gas fired in reduction, cone 10

PHOTO BY MARCUS SKALA

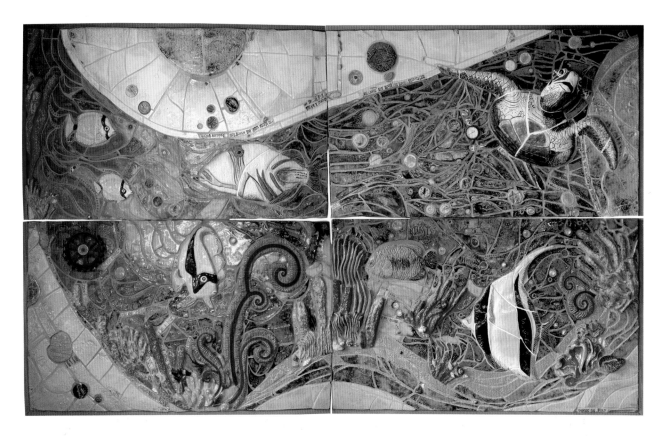

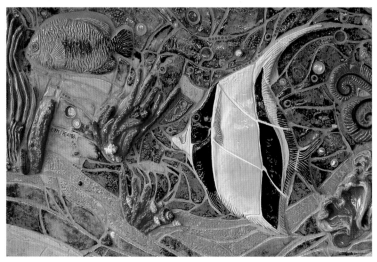

Betsy Kopshina Schulz

Java Kai Mosaic Mural | 2004

120 X 72 INCHES (304.8 X 182.9 CM)

Sculpted tile mosaic; electric fired, cone 5;
rocks, shells, metal, broken tile

PHOTOS BY ARTIST

Stacy Blackmer-Blomquist

Landlocked | 2005

10½ X 11 X 1 INCHES (26.7 X 27.9 X 2.5 CM)

Hand-built stoneware; electric fired,
cone 04; acrylic paint

PHOTO BY WILLIAM BLOMQUIST

Jasna Sokolovic
Waiting | 2007
5¹/₂ X 5¹/₂ X ¹/₄ INCHES (14 X 14 X 0.7 CM)
White earthenware slab; electric fired, cone 06;
glazed, cone 04; stamped, silkscreen printed on wet
clay and bisque; underglaze, glaze, ceramic pencil
PHOTO BY ARTIST

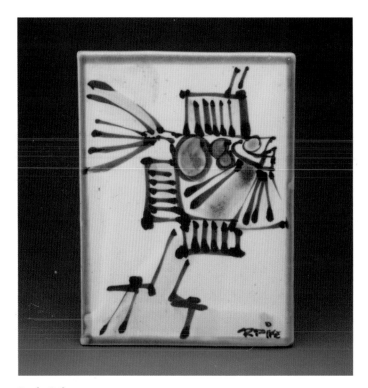

Bob Pike

Fish | 2003

6 X 4 INCHES (15.2 X 10.2 CM)

Buff stoneware; gas fired,
cone 10; overglaze decoration

PHOTO BY ARTIST

Jennifer Victoria Smith
Comfort | 2007
3 1/2 X 5 X 1/4 INCHES (8.9 X 12.7 X 0.6 CM)
White stoneware with underglaze;
electric fired, cone 6
PHOTO BY ANNA V. FREEMAN

Lisa Wolters

Everything's Changed | 2006

14 X 14 INCHES (35.6 X 35.6 CM)

White stoneware; electric fired, underglazes and glazes, cone 6

PHOTO BY BOB WINNER

Terry Nicholas
Fresh Catch | 2006
4 X 8 INCHES (10.2 X 20.3 CM)
Carved porcelain; black slip;
electric fired, cone 6
PHOTO BY ARTIST

Stephen Bird

Entrance to Agacan Restaurant | 2004

86⁵⁄₈ X 59¹⁄₁₆ X 27⁹⁄₁₆ INCHES (220 X 150 X 70 CM)

Wood, cement, stoneware;
electric fired; glazed, cone 10

PHOTOS BY ARTIST

Doug Spalding
Obey | 2006
4³/₄ X 7 INCHES (12 X 17.8 CM)
Raku stoneware fired to 1900°F (1038°C),
decorated with cuerda seca method
PHOTO BY JIM MCCLEAR

David E. Corboy

Oak Leaf | 2006

4⅝ X 4⅜ X ¼ INCHES (11.8 X 11.2 X 0.6 CM)

Press-molded; oxidation fired, cone 6

PHOTO BY LENNY GOTTER
COURTESY OF NORTHFIRE TILE COMPANY

Rosalind Redfern

Copper Red Tile Panel | 2003

31⁷/₈ X 25³/₁₆ X 4¹/₃ INCHES (81 X 64 X 11 CM)

Thrown stoneware; gas fired, cone 10–11; glazed

PHOTO BY WOLFGANG ALTMANN

Vinod Kumar Daroz

Garba-Griha (Temple Series) | 2006

12 X 12 X 1 ¼ INCHES (30.5 X 30.5 X 3.2 CM)

Wheel-thrown stoneware; gas fired, cone 10;
glazed; gold luster fired, 1562°F (850°C)

PHOTO BY ARTIST

Betsy Kopshina Schulz

Java Kai Mosaic Mural | 2004

120 X 72 INCHES (304.8 X 182.9 CM)

Sculpted tile mosaic; electric fired, cone 5;
rocks, shells, metal, broken tile

PHOTOS BY ARTIST

Ed Gates
Cornelia Henderson Gates

Nine Men's Morris | 2006

BOARD: 13¾ X 13¾ X ¾ INCHES (34.9 X 34.9 X 1.9 CM);
TOKENS: 1 X ¼ INCHES (2.5 X 0.6 CM)

Press-molded and slip-painted stoneware; electric
fired, cone 6; mounted on MDO plyboard

PHOTOS BY JUDITH WOOD HENDERSON

Annie McIver

Puriri Moth | 2006

47¼ X 47¼ X ⅜ INCHES (120 X 120 X 1 CM)

Handmade earthenware tiles; electric fired,
1940°F (1060°C); glazed, 2102°F (1150°C)

PHOTO BY JOHN MCIVER

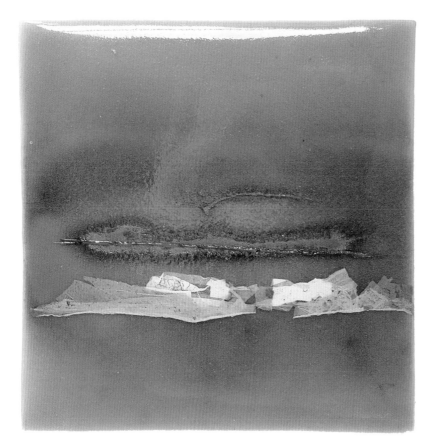

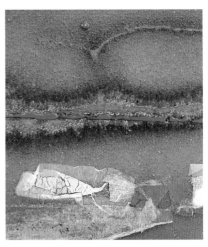

Greg Daly

Decorated Tile with Gold/Silver Leaf and Enamel | 2006

5⁷/₈ X 5⁷/₈ X ⁵/₁₆ INCHES (15 X 15 X 0.8 CM)

Cut stoneware; glaze-on-glaze; gas fired in oxidation, cone 9;
gold and silver leaf, enamel; electric fired, cone 017

PHOTOS BY ARTIST

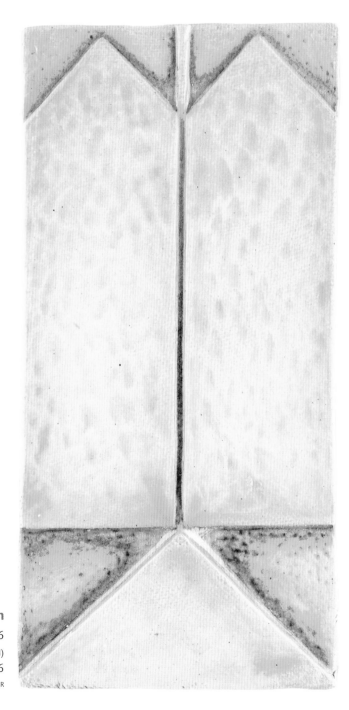

Sandi Langman
Empire | 2006

5 5/8 X 2 13/16 X 1/4 INCHES (16.8 X 18.3 X 0.6 CM)

Press-molded; oxidation fired, cone 6

PHOTO BY LENNY GOTTER

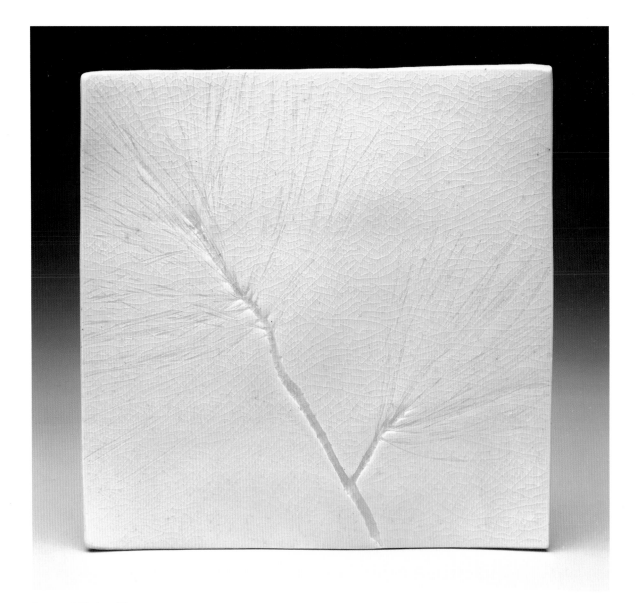

Laura Litvinoff

Pine Tile | 2006

8 X 8 X ⅛ INCHES (20.3 X 20.3 X 0.3 CM)

Hand-cut white stoneware slab; pine branch
impression; clear glaze; reduction fired, cone 10

PHOTO BY JACK REZNICKI

Simon Levin
Window Trivet | 2004
8 X 8 X 1 INCHES (20.3 X 20.3 X 2.5 CM)
Hand-built stoneware with aggregate; impressed
design, inlaid slip; wood fired in anagama kiln, cone 10
PHOTO BY ARTIST

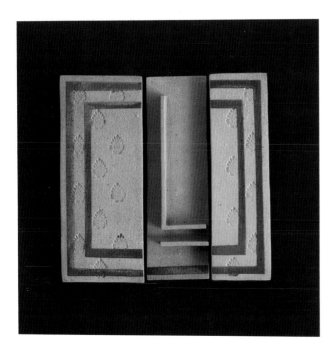

Neha Kudchadkar
Untitled | 2006
12 X 12 X 1¼ INCHES (30.5 X 30.5 X 3.2 CM)
Hand-built stoneware; gas fired,
cone 10; glazed
PHOTO BY MAHESH PADIYA

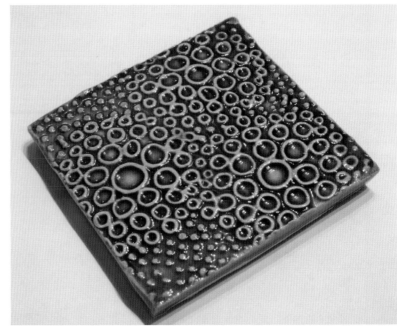

Chloe Vivien Gill
Perene Tiles | 2007
2 X 2 X ¼ INCHES (5 X 5 X 0.7 CM)
Hand-printed Norton grog; electric
fired, cone 06; glazed, cone 1
PHOTO BY ARTIST

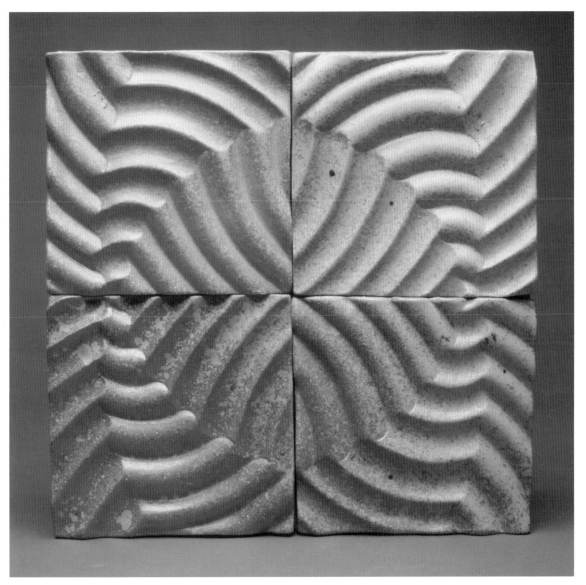

Jeff Brown
Ripple | 2003
13 X 13 X 2 INCHES (33 X 33 X 5.1 CM)
Press-molded and assembled
stoneware; wood fired, cone 10
PHOTO BY CHARLEY FREIBERG

Christine Hibbard

Green Fern | 2006

4 X 4 X ³⁄₄ INCHES (10.2 X 10.2 X 1.9 CM)

Press-molded red clay from hand-carved plaster mold;
electric fired, cone 4; glazed, electric fired, cone 6

PHOTO BY ARTIST

Sara J. Urband-Murphy

Mia | 2004

12 X 7¹/₂ INCHES (30.5 X 19.1 CM)

Sculpted terra cotta; electric fired,
cone 04; glazed, cone 05

PHOTO BY ARTIST

David Ellison

Thistle | 2006

4 X 4 X ⁵/₈ INCHES (10.2 X 10.2 X 1.6 CM)

Press-molded terra cotta; oxidized, cone 04

PHOTO BY PATRICK YOUNG

Carol Gaczek

Wall Flower | 2007

6 X 6 X ¼ INCHES (15.2 X 15.2 X 0.6 CM)

Hand-built and carved stoneware; electric
fired, cone 10, crystalline glaze

PHOTO BY ARTIST

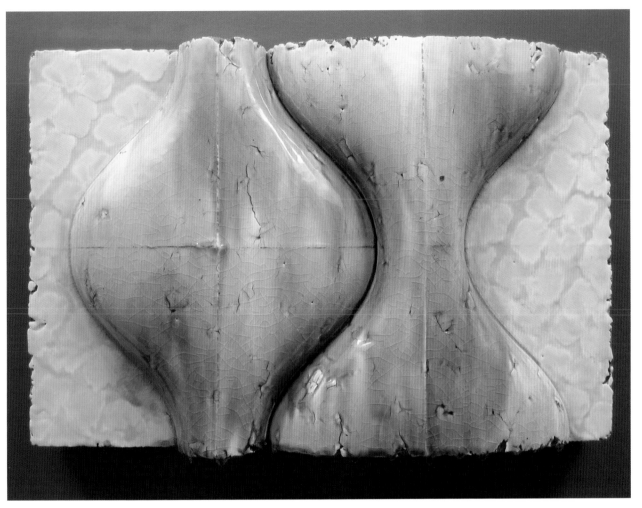

Jason H. Green
Coupling | 2005
13 X 21 X 4 INCHES (33 X 53.3 X 10.2 CM)
Press-molded terra cotta, slip; glaze, cone 04
PHOTO BY ARTIST

Wynne Wilbur
Untitled | 2004
4 X 4 INCHES (10.2 X 10.2 CM)
Maiolica on white earthenware;
electric fired, cone 03
PHOTO BY ARTIST

Elaine Xenelis Fuller

I Am of the Nature to Grow Old. There is No Way to Escape Growing Old | 2006

6 X 6 INCHES (15.2 X 15.2 CM)

Porcelain; underglaze pencil, glaze and glass fired to cone 6 in oxidation

PHOTO BY ARTIST

Shawn Newton
Strawberry Thief | 2007
6 X 6 X ¼ INCHES (15.2 X 15.2 X 0.6 CM)
Porcelain tile mosaic; unglazed
PHOTO BY ARTIST

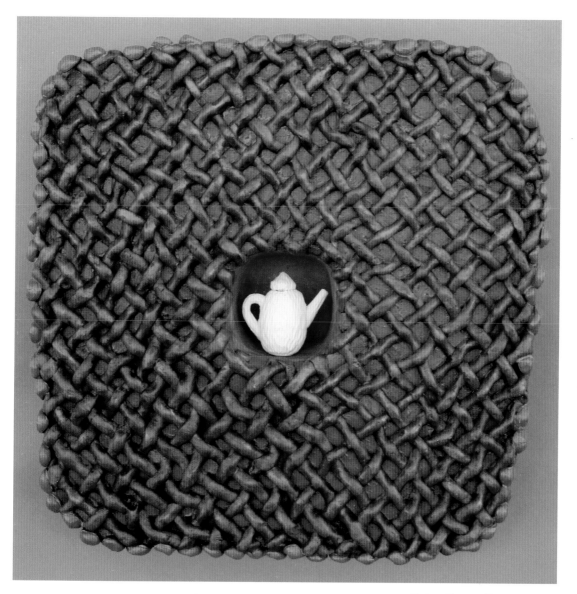

Priscilla Hollingsworth
Teapot Reliquary Woven with Purple | 2007
13 1/2 X 14 X 3 INCHES (34.3 X 35.6 X 7.6 CM)
Hand-built terra cotta; electric fired, glazed, cone 04;
acrylic paint; reduction fired, cone 10

PHOTO BY ARTIST

Dana Burrell
Lady with Duck | 2005
7 1/2 X 6 3/4 X 2 INCHES (19.1 X 17.1 X 5.1 CM)
Hand-built Lizella, Georgia, clay; electric
fired, cone 06; underglaze, cone 2
PHOTO BY DREW STAUSS

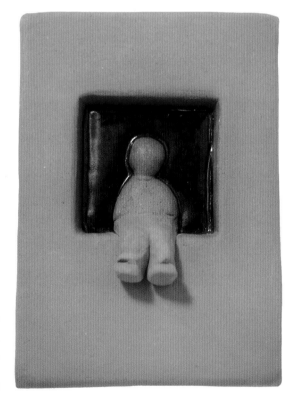

Rosemary Murray
Sitting Boy | 2004
5 1/2 X 4 X 3/8 INCHES (14 X 10.2 X 1 CM)
Terra cotta; electric fired, cone 1
PHOTO BY JO-ANN RICHARDS

Deborah Hecht

Wishing | 2005

6¹/₂ X 8¹/₂ X 1¹/₈ INCHES (16.5 X 21.6 X 2.8 CM)

Press-molded stoneware; electric bisque
fired, cone 04; glaze, cone 5

PHOTO BY ARTIST

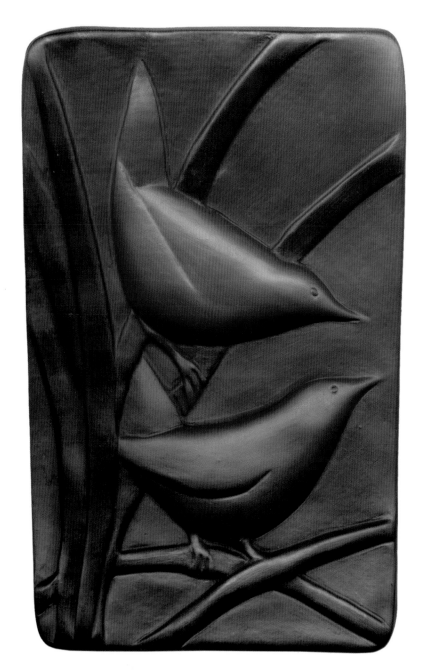

Laura McCaul

Two Wrens in Reeds | 2007

6½ X 4 X ⅜ INCHES (16.5 X 10.2 X 1 CM)

Hand-pressed red earthenware;
terra sigillata; electric fired, cone
06; wood fired in barrel kiln

PHOTO BY ARTIST

Ron Mazanowski

Alpine Locoweed | 2006

18 X 18 X 2 INCHES (45.7 X 45.7 X 5.1 CM)

Earthenware; underglaze, cone 06

PHOTOS BY JANIE WILSON-COOK

Brian J. Boldon
Amy Baur

View from a Distance, Entrance Mural
(detail of facing page) | 2006

40 X 92 X ½ INCH (101.6 X 233.7 X 1.3 CM)

Earthenware; white glaze; laser-printed overglaze enamel
images; oxidation fired, cone 012; handmade kiln-formed
glass tiles full fused, 1450°F (788°C)

PHOTOS BY AMY BAUR / IN PLAIN SIGHT

Ian Dowling

Margaret River Education Campus Waterwall (detail on facing page) | 2004

275 1/8 X 4 3/16 X 2 INCHES (700 X 120 X 5 CM)

Slip cast; glazed; gas fired, cone 6; iron and copper oxides

PHOTOS BY STEPHEN BLAKENEY

Mary-Paige Cannon

Lullaby | 2007

3⁷/₈ X 4¹/₂ X ³/₈ INCHES (9.8 X 11.5 X 1 CM)

White stoneware with underglaze;
electric fired, cone 6

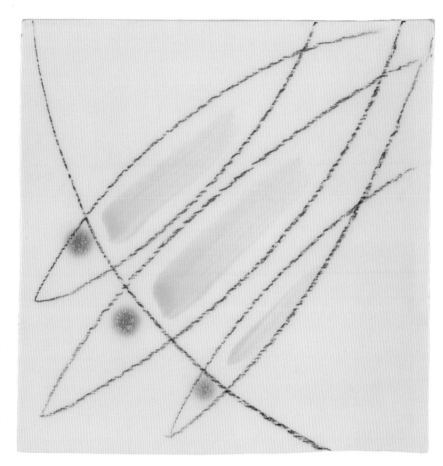

Ursula Sommerer
Fish Tile #2 | 2007
6 1/4 X 6 1/4 X 1/4 INCHES (16 X 16 X 0.6 CM)
Slab-built porcelain; slip and underglaze decoration, clear glaze; electric
fired, cone 6
PHOTOS BY ROGER SMITH

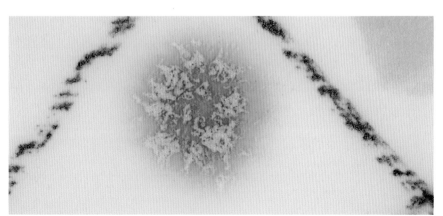

Jasna Sokolovic

Deep | 2007

5 1/2 X 5 1/2 X 1/4 INCHES (14 X 14 X 0.7 CM)

White earthenware slab; electric fired, cone 06; glazed, cone 04; stamped, silkscreen printed on wet clay and bisque; underglaze and glaze

PHOTO BY ARTIST

Lizanne Murison

Protect | 2006

1 3/4 X 4 7/8 X 4 7/8 INCHES (4.5 X 12.5 X 12.5 CM)

Slab-built earthenware, painted slip; mono-printed oxide, glaze; electric fired, cone 2

PHOTO BY HENNIE MEYER

Susan Greenbank

Three Singing Birds | 2007

8 X 8 X 1/4 INCHES (20.3 X 20.3 X 0.6 CM)

Slab-built stoneware; slips, glaze, oxides, bisque cone 6; glaze, reduction fired, cone 10

PHOTO BY LEANNE WILKINSON

Jeanette Harris

Sea Star | 1999

6 X 6 X ½ INCHES (15.2 X 15.2 X 1.3 CM)

Slab-built and sculpted stoneware;
electric fired, cone 6, basic white glaze

PHOTO BY ARTIST

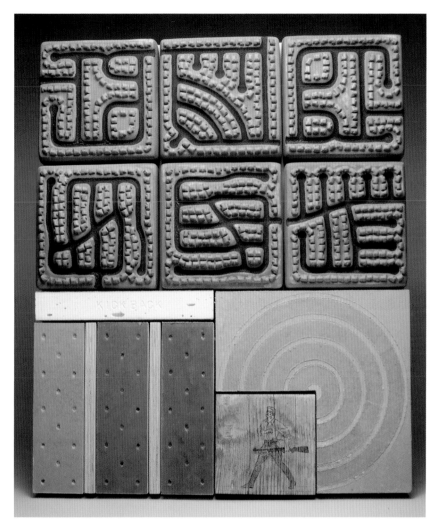

Gary Carlos
Kick Back | 2006
12 X 14 X 2 INCHES (30.5 X 35.6 X 5.1 CM)
Slip cast, low fire; wood,
wallboard, transfer
PHOTO BY ARTIST

Jennifer A. Everett
Tile | 2006
3 X 3 X ³⁄₈ INCHES (7.6 X 7.6 X 1 CM)
Extruded stoneware with
stamped decoration; gas fired
in reduction, cone 10
PHOTO BY ARTIST

Linda Kliewer
Maple Leaves | 2005
18 X 10 INCHES (45.7 X 25.4 CM)
Stoneware; electric fired, cone 5
PHOTO BY COURTNEY FRISSE

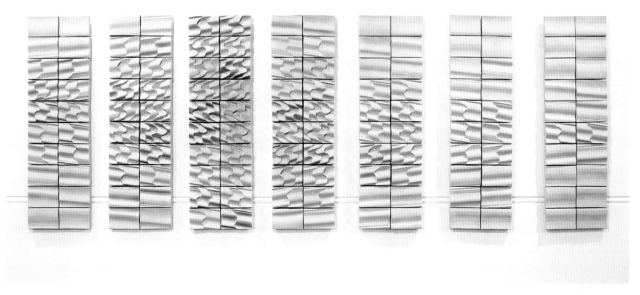

Ian Dowling
Tile Pulse | 2006
47³/₁₆ X 117⁷/₈ X 2³/₄ INCHES (120 X 300 X 7 CM)
Slip cast; glazed; gas fired,
cone 6, copper oxide
PHOTO BY ROBERT FRITH

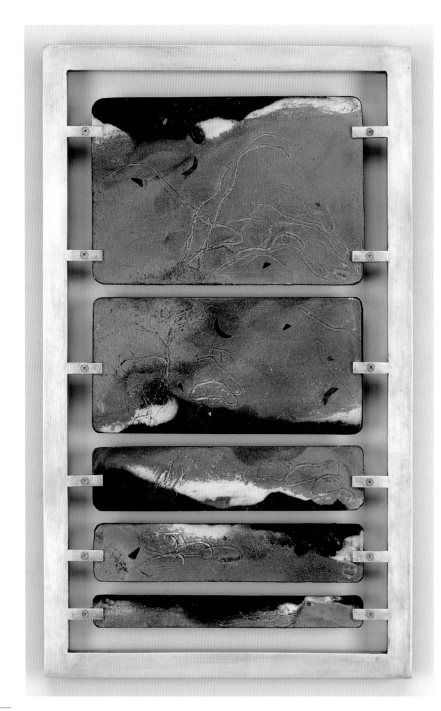

Susan Cohen

Brazos V | 2006

18⁹/₁₆ X 11¹/₄ X 1¹/₄ INCHES (47.1 X 28.6 X 3.2 CM)

Stoneware; glazed and pit-fired; accented with oil paint and silver dust

PHOTO BY MICHAEL LATIL

Bob Pike

Truck | 2003

8 X 8 INCHES (20.3 X 20.3 CM)

Buff stoneware; gas fired,
cone 10; overglaze decoration

PHOTO BY ARTIST

Jonathan Nicklow

Destination | 2006

8 X 8 X ¾ INCHES (20.3 X 20.3 X 1.9 CM)

Low-fire white clay; electric fired, cone 04;
slab-rolled, relief sculpture, stamped
elements, oil paint, tar and varnish

PHOTO BY ARTIST

Beverlee Lehr
Winter Play | 2007
12 X 12 X 2 INCHES (30.5 X 30.5 X 5.1 CM)
Hand-built stoneware; original glazes;
reduction fired, cone 10
PHOTO BY SOCOLOW PHOTOGRAPHY

Colin Johnson
Moonflower II (in darkness) | 2006
54.8 X 82.8 X 4 INCHES (137 X 207 X 10 CM)
Extruded buff clay, slab addition; sprayed
vitreous slip; electric fired, cone 4
PHOTO BY LAMBIE BROTHERS

Colin Johnson
Moonflower | 2005
24 X 24 X 3 $^{15}/_{16}$ INCHES (61 X 61 X 10 CM)
Extruded base, slab-rolled top, buff clay;
vitreous slip; electric fired, cone 4
PHOTO BY ARTIST

Brooks Bouwkamp
Blue Crystalline Tile | 2007
3 3/4 X 3 3/4 X 1/2 INCHES (9.5 X 9.5 X 1.3 CM)
Hand-built white stoneware;
electric fired, cone 10
PHOTO BY DAVE SHERWIN

J. Wesley Allen

Backsplash | 2006

4¹⁄₄ X 4¹⁄₄ INCHES (10.8 X 10.8 CM)

Stoneware; recycled glass; electric fired, cone 07; glaze fired, cone 9–10

PHOTO BY TAKASHI HIROSE

Amanda Dock Martorana

Inspired Industry | 2005–2006

EACH: 10 X 10 X 4 INCHES (25.4 X 25.4 X 10.2 CM)

Slump-molded, hand-carved stoneware, earthenware, and porcelain; fired cone 06–10; glazed, burnished, pit-fired, raku-fired, horse-hair raku; electric fired, cone 6 and 04; gas fired in reduction, cone 9; salt fired, cone 9; wood fired, cone 10

PHOTO BY ARTIST

Karin S. Kraemer

Crazy Room | 2006

18 X 10 X 1 INCHES (45.7 X 25.4 X 2.5 CM)

Hand-built earthenware; hand-mixed maiolica glaze and stain; electric fired, cone 05

PHOTO BY PETER LEE

Mieke van Sambeeck
Untitled | 2006
5³⁄₄ X 5³⁄₄ INCHES (14.5 X 14.5 CM)
Hand-built stoneware; raku fired, cone 06
PHOTOS BY ARTIST

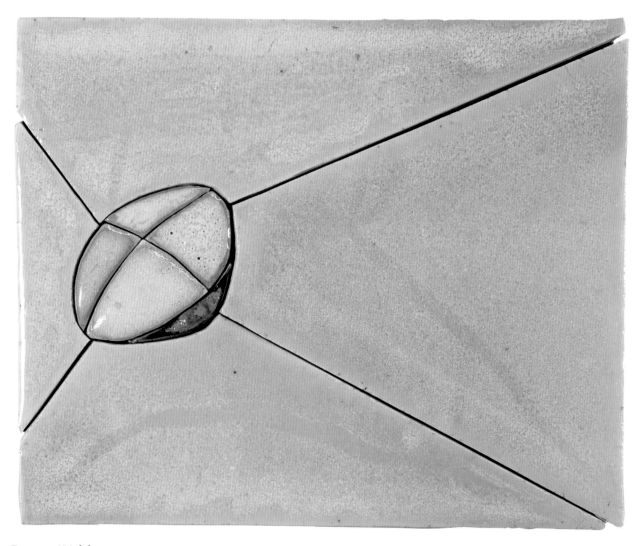

Donna Webb

Crossing | 2006

18 X 22 X 1 INCHES (45.7 X 55.9 X 2.5 CM)

Glazed porcelain; reduction fired, cone 8

PHOTO BY ANDREW MCALLISTER

Tom O'Malley

Green Mountain Vista I | 2006

8 X 4¹/₂ X 2 INCHES (20.3 X 11.4 X 5.1 CM)

Hand-carved porcelain, stoneware holder;
sodium vapor fired, cone 10

PHOTO BY ARTIST

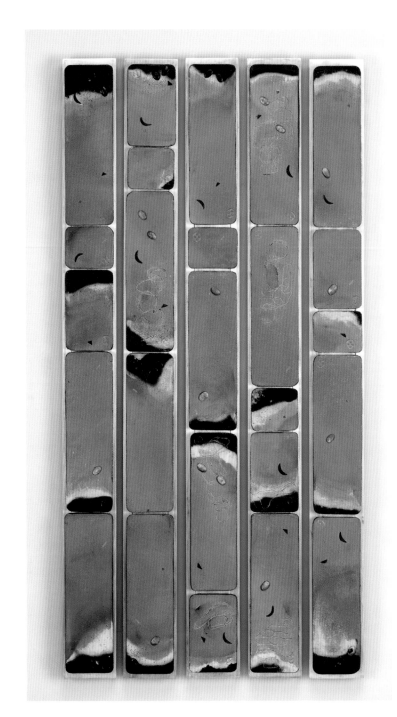

Susan Cohen
Tusas III | 2006
33³/₁₆ X 16¹/₂ X 1¹/₂ INCHES (84.3 X 41.9 X 3.8 CM)
Stoneware; glazed and pit-fired; accented
with oil paint and silver dust
PHOTO BY MICHAEL LATIL

Jodie Atherton
Milk Glass Tiles | 2005
EACH: 4 X 3 ½ X 1 INCHES (10.2 X 8.9 X 2.5 CM)
Hand-carved; electric fired, cone 06; glazed
PHOTO BY ARTIST

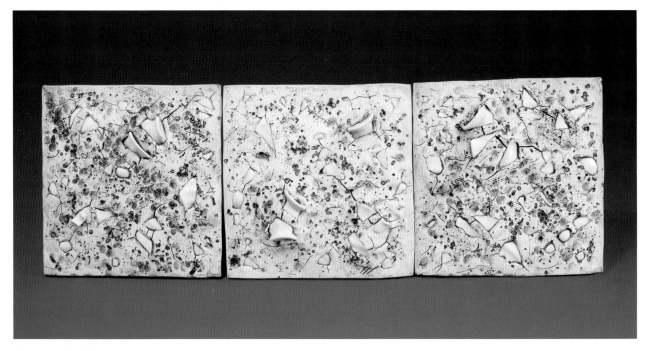

Georgette Zirbes

Manoa Triptych #3 | 2006

9 X 27 X 1 INCHES (22.9 X 68.6 X 2.5 CM)

Press-molded stoneware; slips, glaze fragments,
shards, washes, and transparent glaze; gas fired
in reduction, cone 6

PHOTO BY PATRICK YOUNG

Beverlee Lehr

Fifth Moon | 2007

12 X 12 X 2 INCHES (30.5 X 30.5 X 5.1 CM)

Hand-built stoneware; original
glazes; reduction fired, cone 10

PHOTO BY SOCOLOW PHOTOGRAPHY

Takashi Hirose

Maple Leaf | 2006

5¹/₄ X 5¹/₄ X ¹/₂ INCHES (13.3 X 13.3 X 1.3 CM)

Hand-carved stoneware; electric fired,
cone 07; glaze fired, cone 9–10

PHOTO BY J. WESLEY

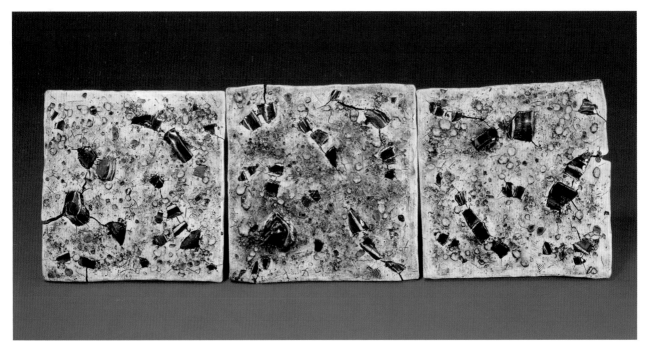

Georgette Zirbes

Timeline Triptych #1 | 2006

9 X 27 X 1 INCHES (22.9 X 68.6 X 2.5 CM)

Press-molded stoneware; slips, glaze fragments, shards, washes, and transparent glaze; gas fired in reduction, cone 6

PHOTO BY PATRICK YOUNG

Jason H. Green

Wall #4 | 2006

54 X 97 X 6 INCHES (137.2 X 246.4 X 15.2 CM)

Press-molded terra cotta with slip transfer
decoration; glaze, cone 04

PHOTOS BY ARTIST

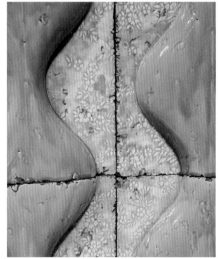

Anat Shiftan

Blue on Orange | 2006

16 X 22 X ½ INCHES (40.6 X 55.9 X 1.3 CM)

Stoneware slab; electric fired,
cone 2; glazed

PHOTO BY ARTIST

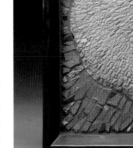

Lisa Wolters

Collaboration | 2005

14 X 14 INCHES (35.6 X 35.6 CM)

Stoneware and raku; electric fired,
stains and glazes, cone 06

PHOTO BY BOB WINNER

Beth Lambert
Triptych | 2006
4¹/₄ X 4¹/₄ X ¹/₄ INCHES (10.8 X 10.8 X 0.6 CM)
Slab-built earthenware with stenciled
slip; electric fired, cone 04
PHOTO BY GEORGE CHAMBERS

Jake McBee

Don Q. Calaveras | 2006

4 X 4 X ½ INCHES (10.2 X 10.2 X 1.3 CM)

Press-molded earthenware; electric fired, cone
06; Brown Sugar gloss glaze, cone 04

PHOTO BY KATHY TOEWS

Kathleen Marie Casper

Suns and Moons | 2006

EACH: 2 X 2 INCHES (5.1 X 5.1 CM)

Slab rolled; electric fired, cone 6;
wax resist design, glazed, cone 6

PHOTO BY LOU TREFZ

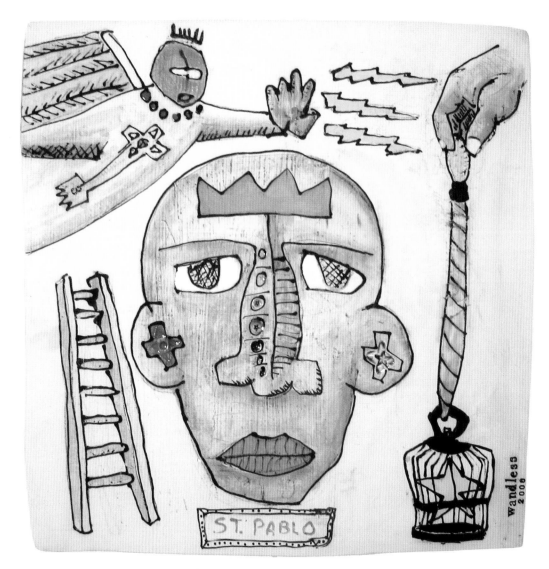

Paul Andrew Wandless

Keeping the Star at Bay #2 | 2006

14 X 14 X ½ INCHES (35.6 X 35.6 X 1.3 CM)

Monotype on white stoneware; electric fired,
cone 04; slips, glaze, cone 04

PHOTO BY ARTIST

Michael C. Hoffman
Sting-Ray Freedom Bike #1 | 2006
4 X 6 X ¼ INCHES (10.2 X 15.2 X 0.6 CM)
Slip-cast stoneware; underglaze transfer
from plaster mold; electric fired, cone
04; glaze fired, cone 04
PHOTO BY ARTIST

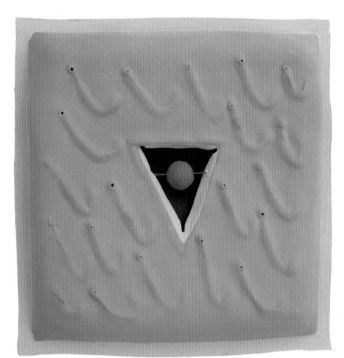

Betsy Cox

Red Ball Number 2 | 2006

12 X 12 X 3 INCHES (30.5 X 30.5 X 7.6 CM)

Press-molded stoneware; electric fired, cone 6; matte glaze, cone 06

PHOTO BY ARTIST

Ted Vogel

Black Sky | 2006

24 X 12 X 2 INCHES (61 X 30.5 X 5.1 CM)

Glazed ceramic, kiln cast and etched glass; cone 07

PHOTO BY ARTIST

Gregory Aliberti
Parmatown Transit Center, G.C.R.T.A. | 2006
EACH: 16 X 16 INCHES (40.6 X 40.6 CM)
Ram-pressed; underglazed, cone 1
PHOTO BY ARTIST

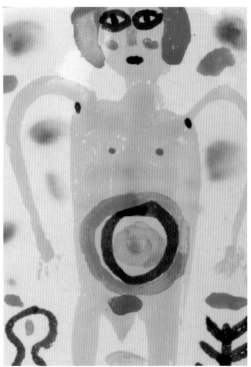

Stephen Bird
Trek in the Himalaya | 2004
22 ¹³/₁₆ X 13 X 6 ⁵/₁₆ INCHES (58 X 33 X 16 CM)
Wood, cement, found objects, earthenware
tiles and figures; electric fired; glazed, cone 1
PHOTOS BY ARTIST

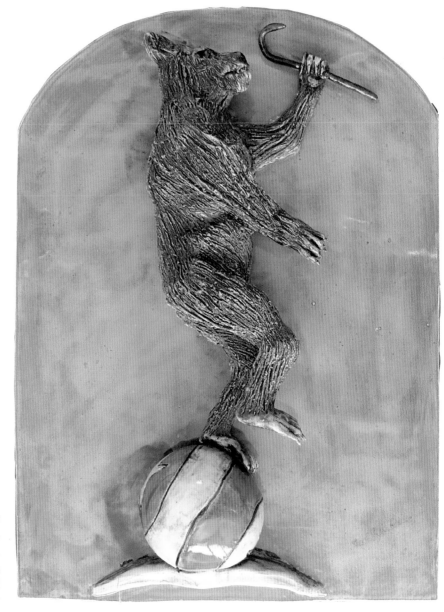

Carol Rose Dean
Dancing Bear | 2006
20 X 14 X ¾ INCHES (50.8 X 35.6 X 1.9 CM)
Newcomb stoneware; mid-range
cone 6; hand-carved
PHOTO BY ARTIST

Catharine Magel
Reflecting on a River | 2003
7 X 22 X 2²/₃ FEET (2.1 X 6.7 X 0.5 METERS)
Hand-sculpted ceramic; cone 6, glazed
PHOTOS BY ARTIST

Betsy Kopshina Schulz
*Solana Beach and Coastal
Rail Trail Entry Arches* | 2006
EACH COLUMN: 48 X 144 INCHES (121.9 X 365.8 CM)
Sculpted tile mosaic; electric fired, cone 5;
rocks, shells, metal, broken tile
PHOTO BY ARTIST

Will Levi Marshall

Wave Wall (detail on facing page) | 2004

78³/₄ X 78³/₄ INCHES (200 X 200 CM)

Low relief slip-cast stoneware blocks; electric fired,
cone 10; glazed, cone 10; platinum luster, cone 018

PHOTOS BY ARTIST

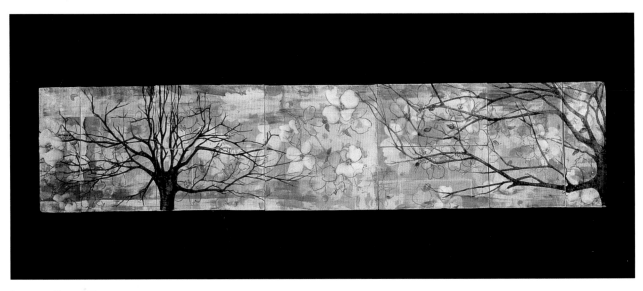

Jacqueline Kierans
Tree #3 | 2007

9¹⁄₂ X 45 X 1 INCHES (24.1 X 114.3 X 2.5 CM)

Press-molded earthenware; electric fired, cone
04; painted and screen printed underglazes;
inglaze Mason stain decals, painted glaze

PHOTO BY GREG STALEY

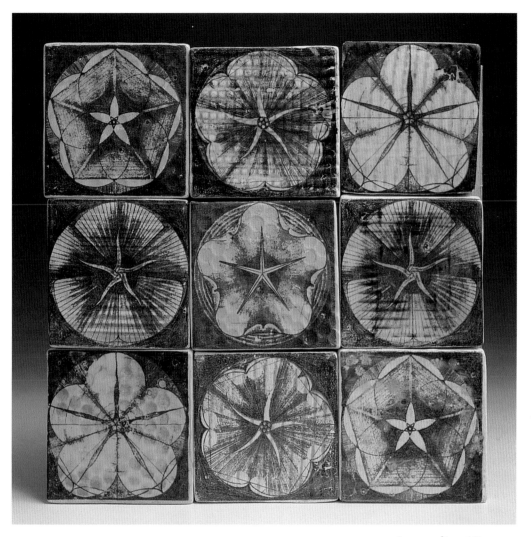

Jacqueline Kierans
Moonflowers | 2006
EACH: 4 X 4 INCHES (10.2 X 10.2 CM)
Earthenware; electric fired, cone 04; stamped
and impressed texture, engobe, mishima;
clear glaze and inglaze Mason stain decal
PHOTO BY GREG STALEY

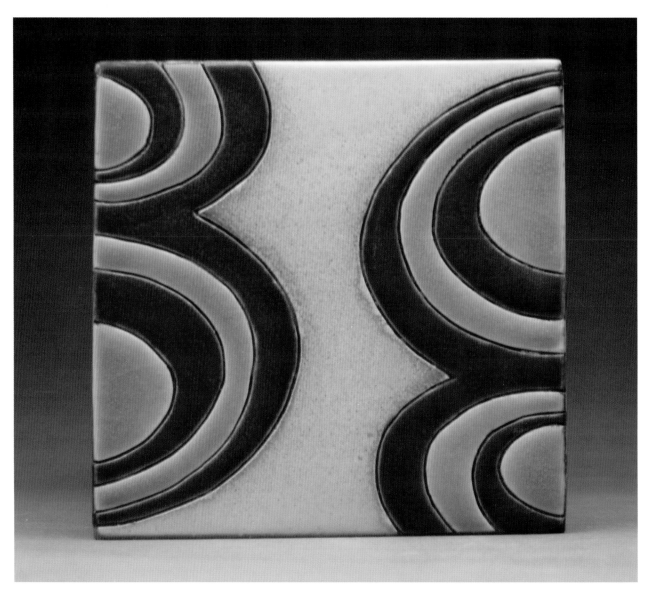

Katie Love
Figure 8 | 2006
4 X 4 INCHES (10.2 X 10.2 CM)
Red stoneware; sgraffito
PHOTO BY ARTIST

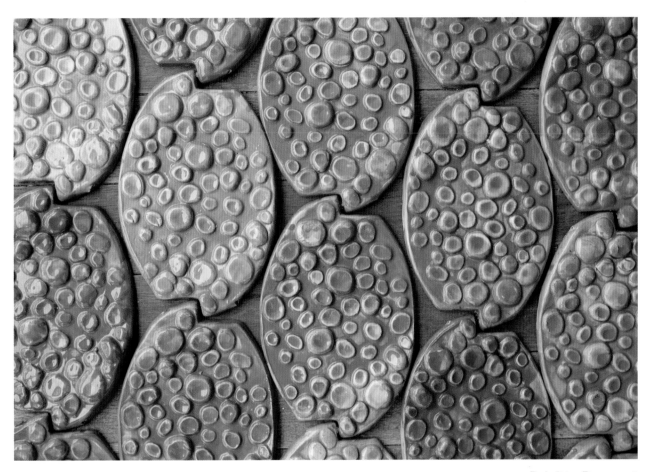

Brigitte Bouquet
Bubbling Wallpaper | 2005
EACH: 3/4 X 5 3/4 X 8 3/4 INCHES (2 X 14.5 X 22 CM)
Press-molded red earthenware; electric
fired, cone 07; glazed, cone 04
PHOTO BY DICK DELANGE

Talia Bensabath

Falling Leaves | 2006

50 X 57 X ¼ INCHES (127 X 144.8 X 0.6 CM)

Press-molded earthenware; electric fired,
cone 04; glazed, cone 06; assembled on
flexible mesh, grouted

PHOTOS BY ARTIST

Fay Jones Day
Tree Lined Road | 2006
6 X 6 X ½ INCHES (15.2 X 15.2 X 1.3 CM)
Terra cotta earthenware; stain;
electric fired, cone 05
PHOTO BY ARTIST

Claudia Riedener

Tortilla (Masa Series) | 2006

18¹⁄₂ X 15 X ¹⁄₂ INCHES (47 X 38.1 X 1.3 CM)

Hand-carved white stoneware; electric
fired, cone 6; Mason stain

PHOTOS BY JOHN CARLTON

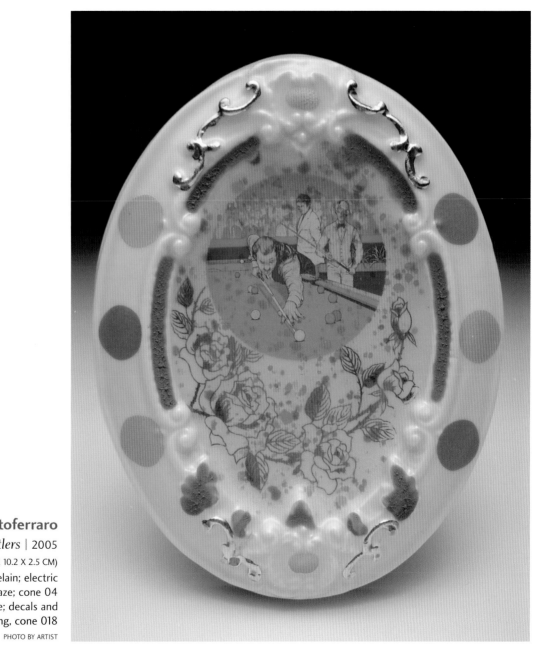

Amy M. Santoferraro
Hustlers | 2005
5 X 4 X 1 INCHES (12.7 X 10.2 X 2.5 CM)
Press-molded porcelain; electric
fired, cone 6 glaze; cone 04
glaze and underglaze; decals and
luster firing, cone 018
PHOTO BY ARTIST

Meredith MacLeod
Nuthatch | 2006
8 X 6 X ¼ INCHES (20.3 X 15.2 X 0.6 CM)
Hand-painted; fused glass tile
PHOTO BY ARTIST

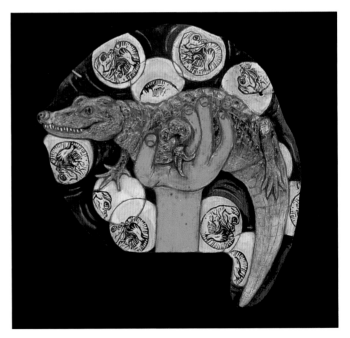

Laura Farrow
Holding 10 - Alligator | 2006
14½ X 13½ X ¾ INCHES (36.8 X 34.3 X 1.9 CM)
Bas-relief earthenware; underglazes,
glazes; raku fired, cold finished
PHOTO BY DIANE AMATO

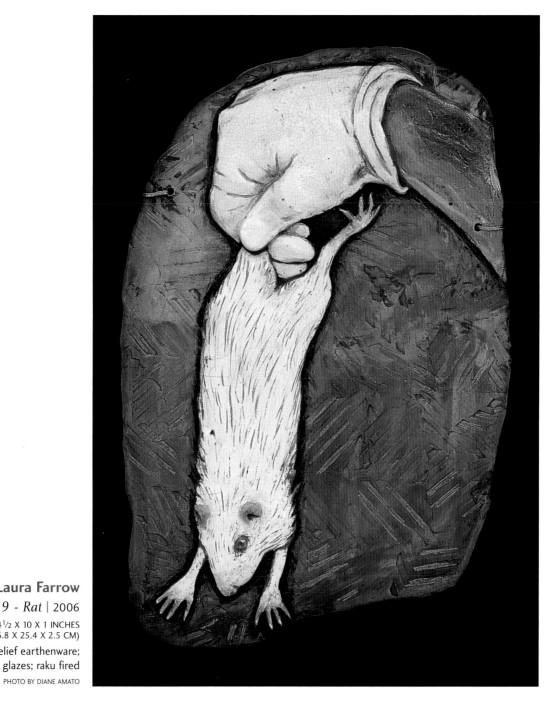

Laura Farrow

Holding 9 - Rat | 2006

14½ X 10 X 1 INCHES
(36.8 X 25.4 X 2.5 CM)

Bas-relief earthenware;
underglazes, glazes; raku fired

PHOTO BY DIANE AMATO

Sarah Raymond

Baby Bottles | 2007

4⁵/₁₆ X 4⁵/₁₆ X 1 INCHES (11 X 11 X 2.5 CM)

Hand-built stoneware; double-walled construction; under-glaze painted with sgraffito drawing; electric fired, cone 6

PHOTO BY VINCE NOGUCHI

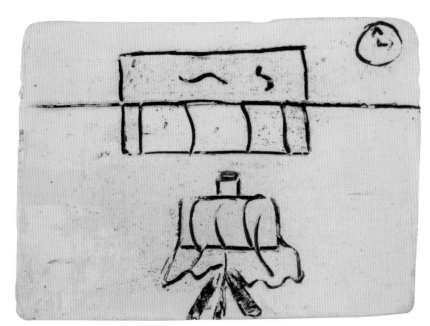

Jennifer Victoria Smith
Flash | 2007
3 1/2 X 5 X 1/4 INCHES (8.9 X 12.7 X 0.6 CM)
White stoneware with underglaze;
electric fired, cone 6
PHOTO BY ANNA V. FREEMAN

Kala Stein
Antiquity Series: Revolver | 2006
9 1/2 X 8 X 3/4 INCHES (24.1 X 20.3 X 1.9 CM)
Slip-cast porcelain; cone 10 reduction
PHOTO BY ARTIST

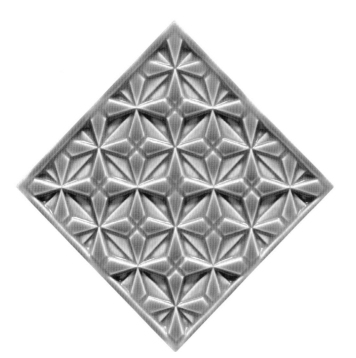

Nielsen Amon
Ruby Levesque
Alhambra | 2006
4 X 4 X ½ INCHES (10.2 X 10.2 X 1.3 CM)
Porcelain; electric fired, cone 6;
transparent flowing glaze, cone 6
PHOTO BY RUBY LEVESQUE

Anat Shiftan
Flower with Blue Dots | 2006
16 X 22 X ½ INCHES (40.6 X 55.9 X 1.3 CM)
Stoneware slab; electric fired, cone 2; glazed
PHOTO BY ARTIST

Simon Levin
Stick Trivet | 2001
8 X 8 X 1 INCHES (20.3 X 20.3 X 2.5 CM)
Hand-built stoneware with inlaid slips;
wood fired in anagama kiln, cone 10
PHOTO BY ARTIST

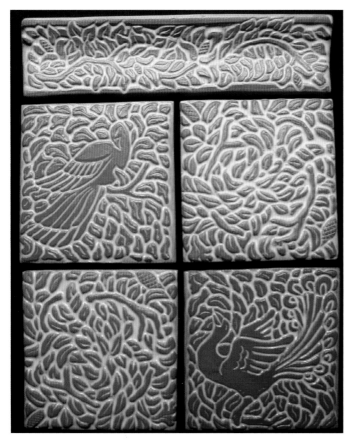

Brian McArthur

New Art Animals | 2004

SHORT TILES: 4 X 4 X ³⁄₈ INCHES (10.2 X 10.2 X 1 CM);
LONG TILE: 8 X 2 X ¹⁄₂ INCHES (20.3 X 5.1 X 1.3 CM))

Hand-pressed terra cotta;
electric fired, cone 04; glaze

PHOTOS BY ARTIST

Nawal Motawi
Karim Motawi
4x12 Calla Lily | 2007
12 X 4 X ⅝ INCHES (30.5 X 10.2 X 1.6 CM)
Press-molded stoneware; electric
fired, cone 04; glazed, cone 6
PHOTO BY JERRY ANTHONY

Scott A. Weaver

Tree Panel with Roots | 2005

34¹⁄₄ X 29¹⁄₄ INCHES (87 X 74.3 CM)

Hand-pressed high-fire stoneware from hand-carved mold; hand-carved white oak; sanded grout; carved and tinted expoxy over grout lines; electric fired, cone 9

PHOTO BY SANDERS VISUAL IMAGES

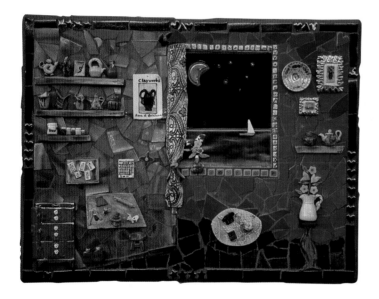

Rose Gispert Quintana
Studio and Room 2 | 2004

19 X 24 X 1 INCHES (48.3 X 61 X 2.5 CM)

Hand-built and sculpted earthenware; bisque fired, cone 04; glazed and under-glazed, cone 06; lusters, cone 018

PHOTOS BY BATIA COHEN

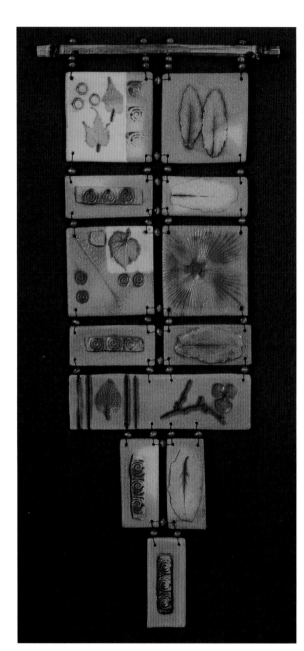

Marianne Kokkoros

Ceramic Tiles Wall Hanging | 2006

27 X 12 INCHES (68.6 X 30.5 CM)

Stoneware; electric fired, cone 6;
underglazes and oxides

PHOTO BY GREGORY R. STALEY

Barry W. Gregg
One Fish Two Fish | 2006
11 ½ X 11 ½ X 1 INCHES (29.2 X 29.2 X 2.5 CM)
Stoneware; electric fired, cone 4;
stains and underglazes, cone 06
PHOTO BY WALKER MONTGOMERY

Randy O'Brien

Shift | 2007

41 X 41 X 2 INCHES (104.1 X 104.1 X 5.1 CM)

Press-molded earthenware; electric fired, cone 03; crawl glaze with Mason stains, cone 05

PHOTO BY WILSON GRAHAM

Marianne Kokkoros
Single Wall Tile | 2006
9 1/2 X 9 1/2 INCHES (24.1 X 24.1 CM)
Stoneware; electric fired, cone 6;
underglazes and oxides
PHOTO BY GREGORY R. STALEY

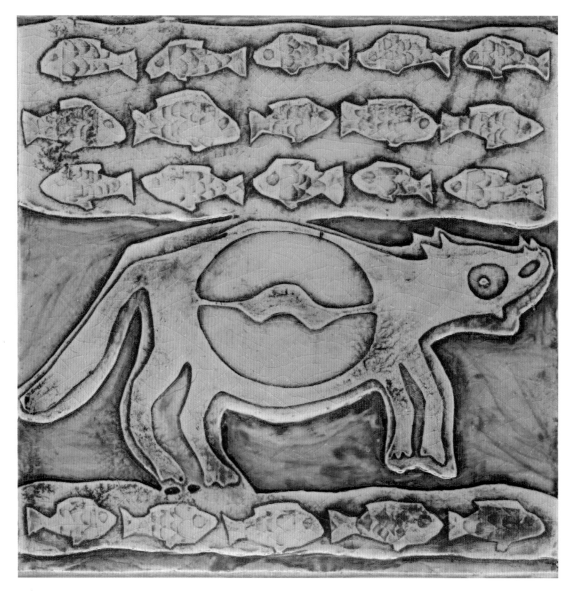

Edwin R. Mighell Jr.
Fox and Fish | 2006
8 X 8 X ⅜ INCHES (20.3 X 20.3 X 1 CM)
Collagraph print on local glacier clay; electric
fired, cone 6; stained and glazed
PHOTO BY ARTIST

Chris Alexiades

Poppy Seed Pods | 2004

5 1/2 X 4 1/2 X 3/8 INCHES (14 X 11.4 X 0.95 CM)

Slab-formed and carved stoneware; raku
fired, cone 04; alligator glaze

PHOTO BY JACK REZNICKI

Shay Amber

Perch 1 | 2006

9 X 9 X 2 INCHES (22.9 X 22.9 X 5.1 CM)

Stiff-slab construction; multi-fired,
cone 016, decal

PHOTO BY STEVE MANN

Shanie Stozek

Papa | 2006

10 X 8 X ¼ INCHES (25.4 X 20.3 X 0.6 CM)

Stoneware; electric fired, cone 6;
terra sigillata, underglaze, silkscreen
photo transfer

PHOTOS BY ARTIST

Haley Mitchem

Do Not Follow | 2007

3 1/2 X 4 1/2 X 1/4 INCHES (8.9 X 11.4 X 0.6 CM)

White stoneware with underglaze;
electric fired, cone 6

PHOTO BY ANNA V. FREEMAN

Ashley Padaon
Perplexity | 2007
4³⁄₄ X 3¹⁄₂ X ¹⁄₄ INCHES
(12.1 X 8.9 X 0.6 CM)
White stoneware with underglaze; electric fired, cone 6
PHOTO BY ANNA V. FREEMAN

Frank Ozereko

Horse | 2005

6 X 6 X 6 INCHES (15.2 X 15.2 X 15.2 CM)

Glaze painted; electric fired, cone 04

PHOTO BY ARTIST

Paula Cooley

L'Amguito Tile #2 | 2006

6¹/₂ X 6¹/₂ X 1¹/₂ INCHES (16.5 X 16.5 X 3.8 CM)

Hand-built stoneware; slip; hand-made
stamps; wood fired, cone 10

PHOTOS BY GRANT KERNAN, AK PHOTOS

Laura Avery
Wild Boar Tile | 2006
8 X 12 X ½ INCHES (20.3 X 30.5 X 1.3 CM)
Hand-carved stoneware; electric fired,
cone 6; hand-painted glazes and stains
PHOTO BY ARTIST

Karen Adelaar
Vulture Tile #46 – "White Bird" | 2003
2 X 9 X 6 INCHES (5.1 X 22.9 X 15.2 CM)
Hand-built tinted porcelain on
stoneware; anagama fired
PHOTO BY STEPHEN GLUCK

Laura Farrow
Holding 1 - Antelope | 2006
13 X 8 X ½ INCHES (33 X 20.3 X 1.3 CM)
Bas-relief earthenware; underglazes, glazes; raku fired
PHOTO BY DIANE AMATO

Betsy Toth
Pam Fletcher
Octet | 2006

8 X 16 INCHES (20.3 X 40.6 CM)

Slab-rolled and hand-cut stoneware;
bisque fired, cone 011; stained and
glazed, electric fired, cone 6

PHOTO BY GREGORY R. STALEY

Jacqueline Kierans
Dogwood Leaves | 2006

5 X 5 X 2 INCHES (12.7 X 12.7 X 5.1 CM)

Press-molded earthenware; electric fired,
cone 04; painted underglaze, screen
printed underglaze, painted glazes

PHOTO BY GREG STALEY

Marcia Reiver

Compass Rose | 2006

2 X 15³/₄ INCHES (5.1 X 40 CM)

Slab-rolled and hand-cut tiles;
raku fired; natural bamboo tray

PHOTO BY JOHN CARLANO

Ruchika Madan

Mosaic Table | 2006

18 X 15 X 15 INCHES (45.7 X 38.1 X 38.1 CM)

Slab-rolled white stoneware; sgraffito and carving; glazed, cone 6; cement board, mastic, grout, wrought iron

PHOTOS BY PAUL DALPÉ

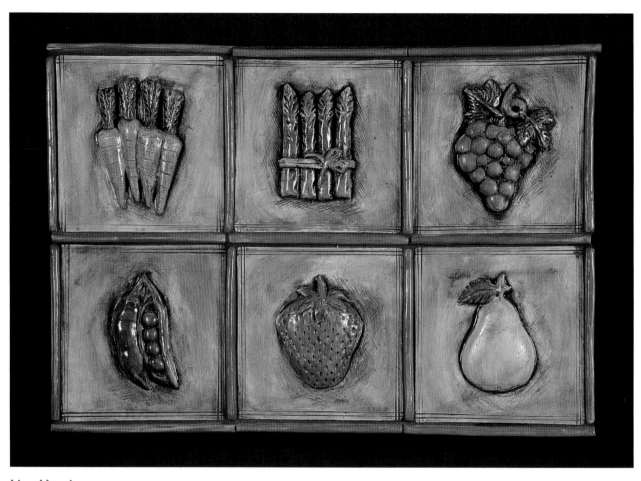

Lisa Harris

Fruit Tile Composition | 2006

13 X 19¹/₂ X ¹/₂ INCHES (33 X 49.5 X 1.3 CM)

Press-molded earthenware; underglaze and glaze; grouted; electric fired, cone 05

PHOTO BY GUY NICOL

Carolyn Ann Kleiner
Rabbit Tile | 2007

10 X 12 X 2 INCHES (25.4 X 30.5 X 5.1 CM)

Hand-carved and sculpted stoneware;
electric fired, cone 6

PHOTO BY ARTIST

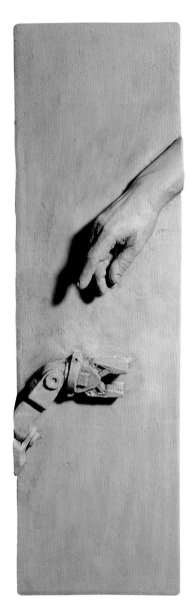

Joseph Mannino

Figurative Relief Tile for Carnegie Mellon Center | 1997

32 X 10 X 6 INCHES (81.3 X 25.4 X 15.2 CM)

Sculpted and press-molded stoneware; glazed, cone 8; gas fired

PHOTO BY ARTIST

Alexandra Powell

Angelic | 2007

17 X 24 X 1 1/8 INCHES (43.2 X 61 X 2.9 CM)

Stoneware; cone 10; stain

PHOTO BY SHARON REAMER

Jamie Lea Johnson
Resting Figure | 2003
48 X 96 X ½ INCHES (121.9 X 243.8 X 1.3 CM)
Glazed; electric fired, cones 06-04; grog, sand
PHOTO BY ARTIST

Miranda Howe

Geometric Landscape | 2006

5 1/2 X 35 X 2 INCHES (14 X 88.9 X 5.1 CM)

Slab-constructed porcelain; soda
and salt fired, cone 10

PHOTOS BY RENNAN REIKE

Susan Cohen
Chaco I | 2006
20¹³/₁₆ X 11 ¹/₈ X 1 ¹/₄ INCHES
(52.9 X 28.3 X 3.2 CM)
Stoneware; glazed and pit-fired;
accented with oil paint, silver
dust, and iron mesh

PHOTO BY MICHAEL LATIL

Ellen Huie
Light Dusting of Snow | 2001
EACH: 6 X 6 INCHES (15.2 X 15.2 CM)
Red earthenware with tile
6 slip; soda fired, cone 04
PHOTO BY SEAN SCOTT

Sara Behling

Fluent Composition | 2006

4 X 2³/₄ X ¹/₁₆ INCHES (10.2 X 7 X 0.2 CM)

Thrown and altered translucent porcelain; electric fired, cone 06; celadon glaze, reduction fired cone 10; downfired; mother-of-pearl luster glaze, cone 018; platinum luster, cone 022

PHOTO BY CHARLIE RAY

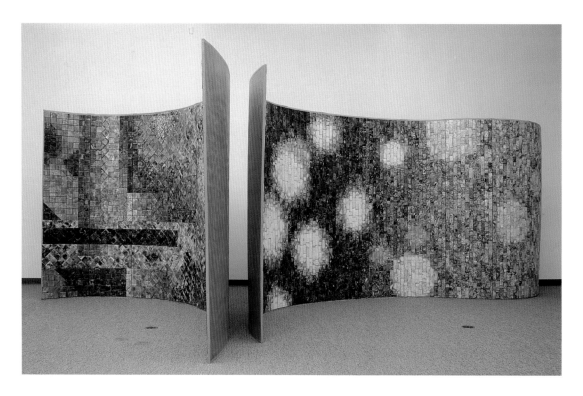

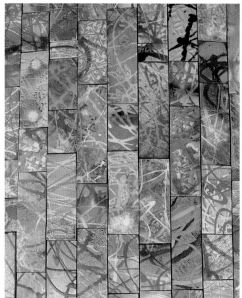

Miranda Howe

*Patterns of Prayer and Creation
- Day 4 - Evening* | 2002

LONGEST: 92 X 134 X 48 INCHES (233.7 X 340.4 X 121.9 CM)

Slab-built terra cotta; electric fired, cone 04; mounted on
wood (Patterns of Prayer), slab-built, embossed, slip-trailed,
silk-screened porcelain, soda and salt fired, cone 6

PHOTOS BY JOSE RIVERA

Lisa Wolters
Shell House | 2006
8 X 10 INCHES (20.3 X 25.4 CM)
Stoneware; electric fired, glazes,
cone 6; shells, glass, tessera
PHOTO BY BOB WINNER

Sharon Bartmann
Mother Nature | 2005
24 X 12 X 1 1/4 INCHES (61 X 30.5 X 3.2 CM)
Press-molded and sculpted
mosaic; raku fired, cone 06
PHOTO BY PEG PETERSON

Rytas Jakimavičius
Bowl | 2006
57 X 47³/₁₆ X 1³/₈ INCHES (145 X 120 X 3.5 CM)
Hand-built earthenware; wood
fired in reduction; recycled tiles
PHOTO BY VIDMANTAS ILLČIUKAS

Sandre Griffin

A Froggy Day | 2006

$5^{5}/_{8}$ X $5^{5}/_{8}$ X $^{3}/_{8}$ INCHES (14.3 X 14.3 X 1 CM)

Slab-rolled white porcelain; black slip and
clear glaze; sgraffito; electric fired, cone 6

PHOTO BY BRYAN JOHNSON

147

Terry Nicholas
Sunday on the St. Johns | 2006
4 X 8 INCHES (10.2 X 20.3 CM)
Carved porcelain; black slip;
electric fired, cone 6
PHOTO BY ARTIST

Gordon Bryan

Handcarved Fish | 1999

6 X 8 X 1 1/2 INCHES (15.2 X 20.3 X 3.8 CM)

Hand-carved and hand-pressed
earthenware; electric fired,
cone 04; glazed, cone 05

PHOTOS BY STEVE BURNS PHOTOGRAPHY

Ruchika Madan
Arch Tile, Bird | 2007
6 X 8 X ³⁄₈ INCHES (15.2 X 20.3 X 1 CM)
Press-molded white stoneware;
sgraffito, slip trailing; glazed, cone 6
PHOTO BY ARTIST

Joseph Mannino

Figurative Relief Tile for Carnegie Mellon Center | 1997

32 X 10 X 6 INCHES (81.3 X 25.4 X 15.2 CM)

Sculpted and press-molded stoneware; glazed, cone 8; gas fired

PHOTO BY ARTIST

Vicki Saulls

California Buckeye | 2002

18 X 18 X ½ INCHES (45.7 X 45.7 X 1.3 CM)

Hand press–molded low-fire clay; gas fired bisqueand glaze, cone 06

PHOTO BY TOM SEAWELL

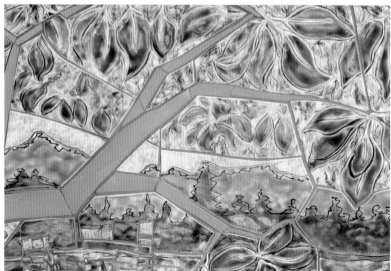

Rosemary Murray
The View from Thetis Island | 2005
60 X 63 X ¼ INCHES (152.4 X 160 X 0.6 CM)
Terra cotta and white clay; electric fired, cone 1, alkaline glaze
PHOTOS BY JO-ANN RICHARDS

Debra Felix

Dragonfly Tile | 2006

8 X 6 X ½ INCHES (20.3 X 15.2 X 1.3 CM)

White earthenware; texture
stamping; electric fired, cone 05;
painted with crackle glazes

PHOTO BY ARTIST

Shay Amber

Digging in the Dirt | 2006

9 X 9 X 2 INCHES (22.9 X 22.9 X 5.1 CM)

Stiff-slab construction;
multi-fired, cone 016, decal

PHOTO BY STEVE MANN

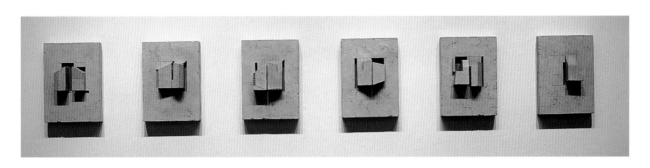

Nicholas Wood

Tablets - Exteriors #8 | 2002

16 X 86 X 4¹/₂ INCHES (40.6 X 218.4 X 11.4 CM)

Press-molded and carved terra cotta;
electric fired, cone 04; glazed, cone 04

PHOTOS BY ARTIST

Rick Nickel

Cars Men Drive | 2006

9 X 9 X 1 INCHES (22.9 X 22.9 X 2.5 CM)

Earthenware; electric fired;
engobes, cone 04

PHOTO BY ARTIST

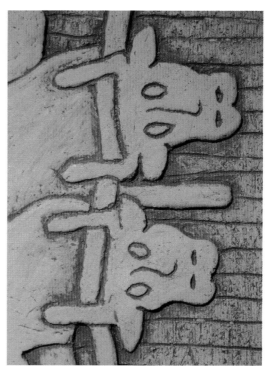

Claudia Riedener

Plow (Masa Series) | 2006

18 1/2 X 15 X 1/2 INCHES (47 X 38.1 X 1.3 CM)

Hand-carved white stoneware; electric fired, cone 6; Mason stain

PHOTOS BY JOHN CARLTON

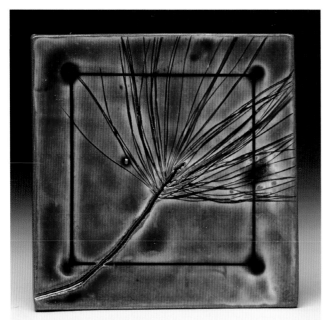

Laura Litvinoff
Pine Tile | 2006
3 X 3 X ⅛ INCHES (7.6 X 7.6 X 0.3 CM)
Hand-cut white stoneware slab;
pine branch impression; temmoku
glaze; reduction fired, cone 10
PHOTO BY JACK REZNICKI

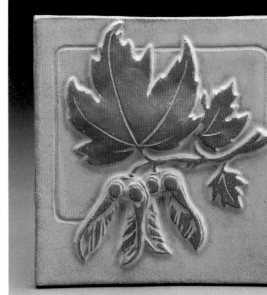

Yancey Crafted Tile, Inc.
Living Canopy - Oak | 2006
6 X 6 INCHES (15.2 X 15.2 CM)
Press-molded terra cotta; electric fired,
cone 05; glazed dark ochre, cone 04
PHOTO BY ARTIST

Linda Boston
Royal Oak Outdoor Art Fair Tile | 2000
4¹/₄ X 4¹/₄ X ¹/₂ INCHES (10.8 X 10.8 X 1.3 CM)
Press-molded stoneware; electric bisque fired,
cone 06; oxidation glazed, cone 9
PHOTO BY JOSEPH KUGIELSKY

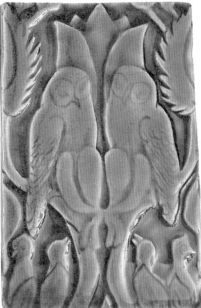

Vicki L. Helber
Owl Tapestry | 2001
6 X 6 X ½ INCHES (15.2 X 15.2 X 1.3 CM)
Hand-carved and press-molded
white sculpture clay; electric
fired, cone 04; glazed, cone 05
PHOTO BY DANIELLE URSCHEL

Katie Love
Quatrefoil Trivet | 2006
13 X 13 X 1 ½ INCHES (33 X 33 X 3.8 CM)
Red stoneware; sgraffito
PHOTO BY ARTIST

Betsy Toth
Pam Fletcher
Zen Woods | 2006
11 X 16 INCHES (27.9 X 40.6 CM)
Slab-rolled and hand-cut
stoneware; bisque fired, cone 011;
stained, electric fired, cone 4
PHOTO BY GREGORY R. STALEY

Stephen Horn

Above and Below | 2006

10¹/₂ X 10 X 1¹/₂ INCHES (26.7 X 25.4 X 3.8 CM)

Hand-built stoneware, photocopy
toner print; gas fired, cone 5; glaze,
cone 5; steel frame

PHOTO BY SCOTT BRINEGAR

Lisa Harris

Urban Landscape | 2006

13 X 17¹/₂ X ¹/₄ INCHES (33 X 44.5 X 0.6 CM)

Hand-painted bisque with glazes;
electric fired, cone 05

PHOTOS BY GUY NICOL

Kina Crow

They Only Come Out at Night | 2007

8 X 8 X ½ INCHES (20.3 X 20.3 X 1.3 CM)

Hand-built mid-fired stoneware; toner
transfer of digitized images; underglaze,
glaze, luster; multifired in electric kiln;
copper wire and acrylic post firing

PHOTO BY ARTIST

Melody Ellis
Dog-Faced Boy | 2006
5 1/2 X 4 3/4 X 1 1/2 INCHES (14 X 12.1 X 3.8 CM)
Hand-carved earthenware; slips and
underglazes, cone 04; glazes, cone 05
PHOTO BY ARTIST

Ian F. Thomas

5000:1 | 2007

8 X 10 X 1½ INCHES (20.3 X 25.4 X 3.8 CM)

Carved and etched earthenware and terra cotta; electric fired, cone 04; graphite

PHOTO BY ARTIST

Ruchika Madan
Tool Tile Trio | 2006
EACH: 4 X 4 X ⅜ INCHES (10.2 X 10.2 X 1 CM)
Press-molded white stoneware;
sgraffito; glazed, cone 6
PHOTO BY ARTIST

Brian Jensen
Bug Tiles | 2001
40 X 38 INCHES (101.6 X 96.5 CM)
Stoneware; screen-printed
images; bisque fired, cone 08;
clear glaze, cone 04
PHOTO BY ARTIST

Haley Mitchem
Snap, Crackle, Pop | 2007
3 1/4 X 4 1/2 X 1/4 INCHES (8.3 X 11.4 X 0.6 CM)
White stoneware with underglaze;
electric fired, cone 6
PHOTO BY ANNA V. FREEMAN

Lizanne Murison

Synchronicity | 2006

EACH: 1 3/4 X 4 7/8 X 4 7/8 INCHES (4.5 X 12.5 X 12.5 CM)

Slab-built earthenware, painted slip; mono-
printed oxide, glaze; electric fired, cone 2

PHOTO BY HENNIE MEYER

Sumner R. Bradshaw
*Where Do You Want To Go
Today? (Part 1)* | 2007
5 1/2 X 5 1/2 X 1/4 INCHES (14 X 14 X 0.6 CM)
White stoneware with underglaze;
electric fired, cone 6
PHOTO BY ANNA V. FREEMAN

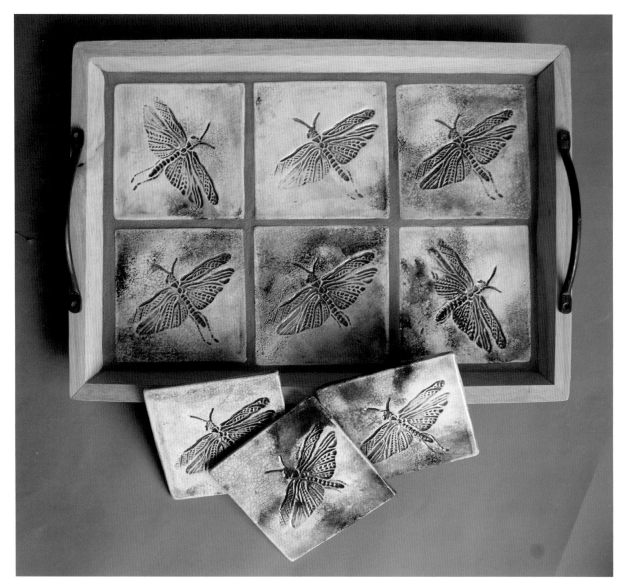

Jodie Atherton

Locust Serving Tray | 2005

EACH TILE: 6 X 6 X ¼ INCHES (15.2 X 15.2 X 0.6 CM)

Hand-stamped with original locust design;
electric fired, cone 06; glaze, pit-fired

PHOTO BY ARTIST

Miranda Howe
Elements of Process | 2006
22 X 16 X 3 1/2 INCHES (55.9 X 40.6 X 8.9 CM)
Slab-constructed white stoneware, porcelain,
wadding; soda and salt fired, cone 10
PHOTO BY RENNAN REIKE

Terry Nicholas
Fish Fountain | 2002
54 INCHES (137.2 CM)
Slab-built; mosaic inserts;
electric fired, cone 6
PHOTO BY ARTIST

Susan Wink

Creative Learning Center Mosaic Mural | 2005

13 X 24 FEET (396.2 X 731.5 CM)

Handmade and glazed bisque
commercial tile; electric fired, cone 6

PHOTOS BY NANCY FLEMING

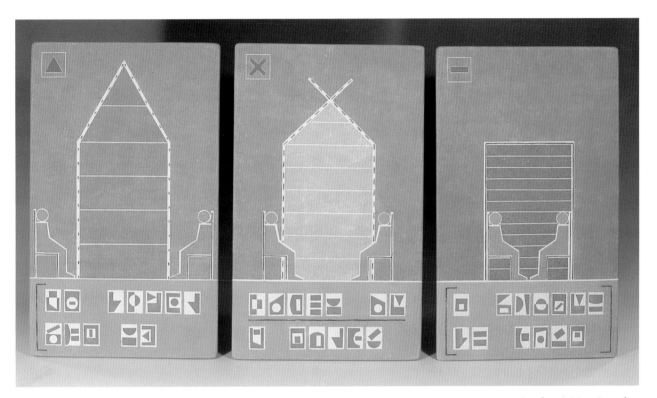

Andrew VanAssche

Secure, Undisclosed | 2005

EACH: 13 1/2 X 8 3/8 X 3/8 INCHES (34.3 X 21.3 X 1 CM)

Slab-rolled stoneware; oxidation fired, cone 4;
clay slips and underglaze decoration

PHOTO BY ARTIST

Chloë Marr-Fuller
Two Houses | 2006
EACH: 3 X 1³⁄₄ INCHES (7.6 X 4.4 CM)
Slab-rolled terra cotta; electric
fired, cone 04; carved, glazed
PHOTO BY MONICA RIPLEY

Dorothy H. Segal

"Allons! The road is before us..." | 2006

7³/₄ X 7¹/₄ X ³/₈ INCHES (19.7 X 18.4 X 1 CM)

Press-molded terra cotta with hand-cut
stamps; glazed; electric fired, cone 04

PHOTOS BY ARTIST

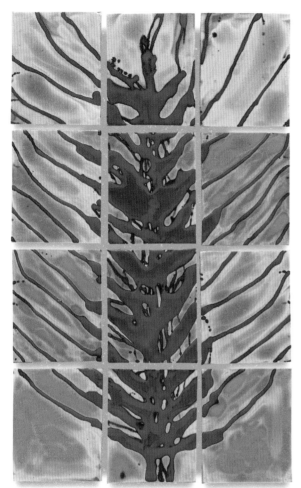

Josh Blanc

Blossfeldt Barley | 2005

EACH: 4 X 3 X 1 INCHES (10.2 X 7.6 X 2.5 CM)

Handmade glazed terra cotta; electric fired, cone 04; commercial glazes

PHOTO BY DIGIGRAPHICS-PHOTOS INC.

Paul A. McCoy

Riverbed Series #4 | 2003

11 1/2 X 11 1/2 X 1 3/4 INCHES (29.2 X 29.2 X 4.4 CM)

Ram-pressed, altered stoneware with deflocculated slips; gas fired, reduction fired, cone 6

PHOTO BY BOB SMITH

John Heaney
Tile | 2006
13³⁄₈ X 9⁷⁄₁₆ X 1³⁄₁₆ INCHES (34 X 24 X 3 CM)
Wire cut slab, Rye's Soda Feldspar
stoneware; ash melt; wood fired, cone 13
PHOTO BY STEWART HAY

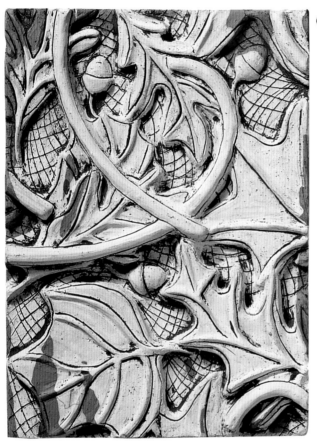

Nancy McCroskey

Botanica | 2005

11 X 18 X 1 INCHES (27.9 X 45.7 X 2.5 CM)

Press-molded earthenware, poured white slip and sgrafitto on green clay, electric fired, cone 04; stain, cone 05

PHOTO BY ARTIST

Vicki Saulls

California Poppy | 2002

18 X 18 X¹/₂ INCHES (45.7 X 45.7 X 1.3 CM)

Hand press-molded low-fire clay; gas
fired bisque and glaze, cone 06

PHOTO BY TOM SEAWELL

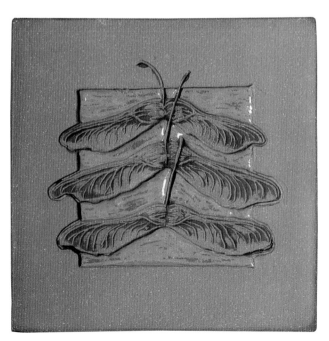

Linda S. Leighton

Winged Maple Seeds | 2006

5 X 5 X ¹/₂ INCHES (12.7 X 12.7 X 1.3 CM)

Carved stoneware; oxidation fired,
cone 05; underglazes and glazes,
cone 6

PHOTO BY TERRY TALBOT

Barbara Duncan Tipton

Copper River Chickadees | 2006

8 X 20 X ½ INCHES (20.3 X 50.8 X 1.3 CM)

Hand-cut earthenware clay; sculpted, textured; electric fired, cone 04; hand-painted in under-glaze; glazed, fired, grouted

PHOTOS BY WILLIAM DUNCAN TIPTON

Susan Wink
Curios | 2003
EACH: 6 1/8 X 6 1/8 X 3/4 INCHES (15.5 X 15.5 X 1.9 CM)
White stoneware; glaze and underglaze;
electric fired, cone 6
PHOTO BY JOSE RIVERA

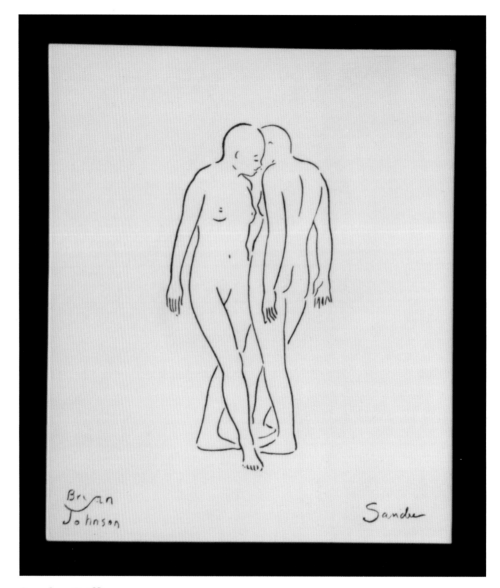

Sandre Griffin
Bryan Johnson
The Dance | 2006
13 1/4 X 11 1/4 X 1/4 INCHES (33.7 X 28.6 X 0.6 CM)
Slab-rolled porcelain with inlay; clear glaze; electric fired, cone 6
PHOTO BY BRYAN JOHNSON

Kala Stein
Phrenological Map of the Head | 2006
5.5 X 5.5 X 1 INCHES (14 X 14 X 2.5 CM)
Slip-cast porcelain; cone 10 reduction;
laser printed decal, cone 05 oxidation
PHOTO BY ARTIST

Frank Ozereko

4 Dogs | 2006

6 X 6 X 6 INCHES (15.2 X 15.2 X 15.2 CM)

Glaze painted; electric fired, cone 04

PHOTO BY ARTIST

Melanie Ann Wegner
Border Tiles - Dancing Day of the Dead | 2006
24 X 4 INCHES (61 X 10.2 CM)
Press-molded earthenware;
glazed; electric fired, cone 04
PHOTO BY MARGOT GEIST

Laura McCaul

Two Goldfinches | 2007

6 1/2 X 4 X 3/8 INCHES (16.5 X 10.2 X 1 CM)

Hand-pressed red earthenware; terra sigillata; electric fired, cone 06; wood fired in barrel kiln

PHOTO BY ARTIST

Kina Crow

They Call Me Mama Crow | *2007*

7 X 7 X ½ INCHES (17.8 X 17.8 X 1.3 CM)

Hand-built mid-fired stoneware; glass frit,
toner transfer of digitized image; slips,
glaze, luster; multi-fired in electric kiln

PHOTO BY ARTIST

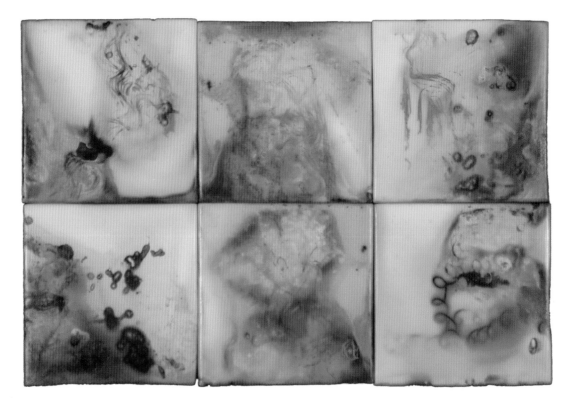

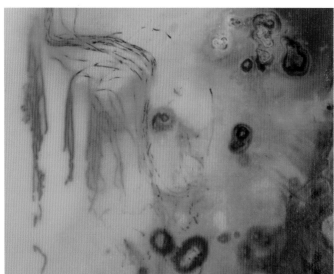

Pamela Timmons
Beachwalking | 2006
16 X 24 INCHES (40.6 X 61 CM)
Press-molded stoneware tiles;
fumed to 1600°F (871°C)
PHOTOS BY JIM WOLNOSKY

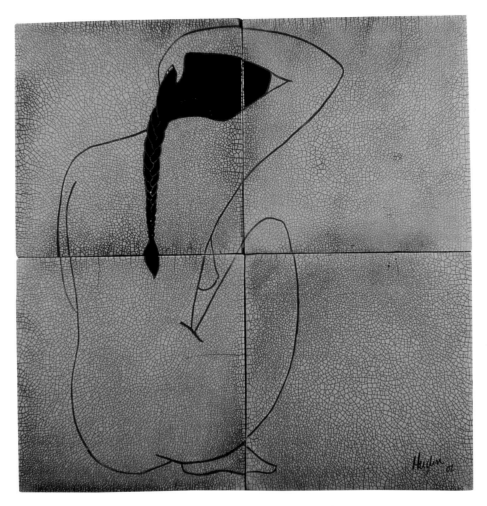

Cathryn R. Hudin
Braided Hair | 2002
24 X 24 X 1 INCHES (61 X 61 X 2.5 CM)
Raku clay; raku fired, cone 05;
hand drawn; artists' glazes

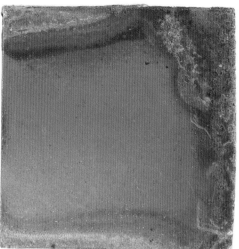

Darren L. Cockrell

Shower Tiles | 2007

EACH: 6 X 6 X ¾ INCHES (15.2 X 15.2 X 1.9 CM)

Slab-rolled and hand-cut stoneware;
wood-fired, natural ash and shino
glazes, cone 12

PHOTO BY DONALD J. FELTON

Ian F. Thomas

Now and Later | 2007

12 X 9 X 1½ INCHES (30.5 X 22.9 X 3.8 CM)

Carved and etched earthenware;
electric fired, cone 04; graphite

PHOTO BY ARTIST

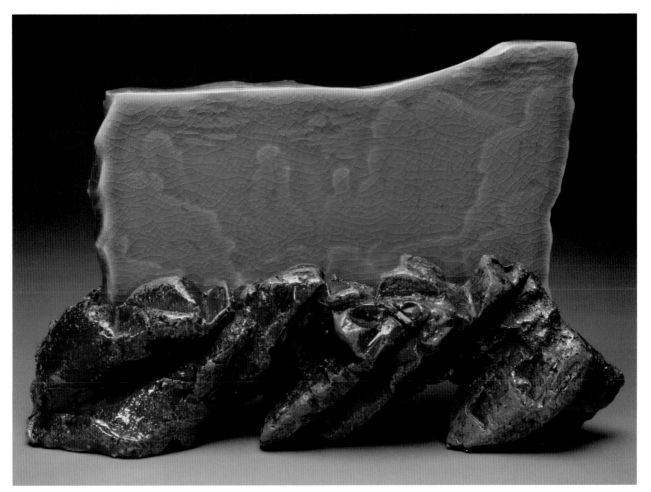

Tom O'Malley

Green Mountain Vista II | 2006

6 X 9 X 2 INCHES (15.2 X 22.9 X 5.1 CM)

Hand-carved porcelain, stoneware
holder; sodium vapor fired, cone 10

PHOTO BY ARTIST

John Heaney

Tile | 2006

10¹/₄ X 13³/₈ X 1³/₁₆ INCHES (26 X 34 X 3 CM)

Slab-built Rye's Soda Feldspar
stoneware; wood fired, unglazed

PHOTO BY STEWART HAY

Dryden Wells
Untitled | 2006
4 X 7 X ¼ INCHES (10.2 X 17.8 X 0.6 CM)
Hand-rolled stoneware; black
oxide wash; subtractive drawing,
reduction fired, cone 6
PHOTO BY WES HARVEY

Melanie Ann Wegner

Border Tiles - Rabbit | 2003

24 X 4 INCHES (61 X 10.2 CM)

Press-molded earthenware; glazed;
electric fired, cone 04

PHOTO BY MARGOT GEIST

Anne Lloyd
Ponies | 1993
13 X 8¹/₂ INCHES (33 X 21.6 CM)
Raku, bas-relief; clear and
copper matte raku glazes

PHOTO BY JOHN CARLANO

Beverly Crist

NoHo Mural (Woman, Juggler, Bear) | 2002

31 X 54 INCHES (78.7 X 137.2 CM)

Hand-modeled earthenware with underglazes;
electric fired, cone 04 bisque and glaze

PHOTO BY SHARON GOTOLA

John Wehrle
Rescue | 2005
96 X 120 INCHES (243.8 X 304.8 CM)
Commercial 12-inch (30.5 cm)
terra-cotta pavers; glazed,
electric fired, cone 04
PHOTO BY ARTIST

Skuja Braden

*Skuja Braden: Artists'
Double Portrait* | 2005

14 X 9 X ⅕ INCHES (35.6 X 22.9 X 0.5 CM)

Slab-rolled porcelain; electric fired, cone
4; glazed and stained inscribed design,
cone 6; gold luster, cone 018

PHOTO BY TONY NOVOLOZO

Kina Crow
Safety of the Nest | 2007
7 X 7 X ½ INCHES (17.8 X 17.8 X 1.3 CM)
Hand-built stoneware; toner transfer
of digitized image; multi-fired in
electric kiln; copper wire
PHOTO BY ARTIST

Anne Gregerson
Garden Moment | 2006
9 X 6 X 1 INCHES (22.9 X 15.2 X 2.5 CM)
Press-molded stoneware; electric fired,
cone 04; underglazed, cone 04;
transparent matte glaze, cone 06
PHOTO BY DAVID HAWKINSON

Jenny Mendes

Lovely Fruit | 2006

11 X 8¹/₂ X ¹/₄ INCHES (27.9 X 21.6 X 0.6 CM)

Hand-rolled earthenware slab; terra sigillata
with sgraffito; electric fired, cone 03

PHOTO BY TOM MILLS

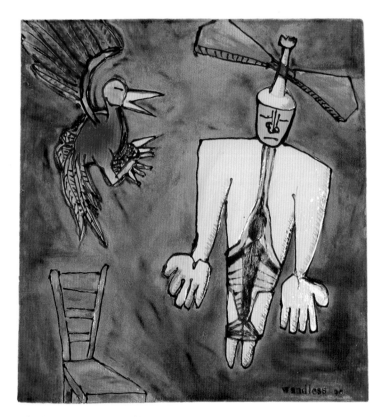

Paul Andrew Wandless

Flyer | 2006

14 X 14 X ½ INCHES (35.6 X 35.6 X 1.3 CM)

Monotype, linocut embossed on
white stoneware; electric fired,
cone 04; slips, glaze, cone 04

PHOTO BY ARTIST

Kathleen Marie Casper
Lady Guadalupe | 2006
6 X 6 INCHES (15.2 X 15.2 CM)
Slab rolled; electric fired, cone 6;
wax resist design, glazed, cone 6
PHOTO BY LOU TREFZ

Shawn Newton
Lady with Flower | 2006
12 X 12 X ¼ INCHES (30.5 X 30.5 X 0.6 CM)
Porcelain tile mosaic; unglazed
PHOTO BY ARTIST

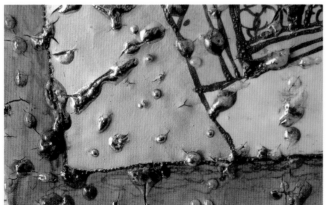

Rimas VisGirda

Frederick's SF650-1 | 2006

10½ X 11 X 1½ INCHES (26.7 X 27.9 X 3.8 CM)

Slab-rolled porcelain with granite;
natural edges, slip-trailed drawing;
underglaze pencil; electric fired,
cone 10; lusters, cone 017

PHOTOS BY ARTIST

The tile reads: "be side Peaceful water, filled with much Sun light, joy and love. My life is better than anything I can dream. I have found a lovely home"

Diane R. Husson

Beach House Paradise | 2006

24 X 37 X 2 INCHES (61 X 94 X 5.1 CM)

Hand-built earthenware; underglaze colors and engobes; electric fired, cone 03; glazed, cone 06; gold overglaze, cone 017

PHOTO BY EMILE B. HUSSON

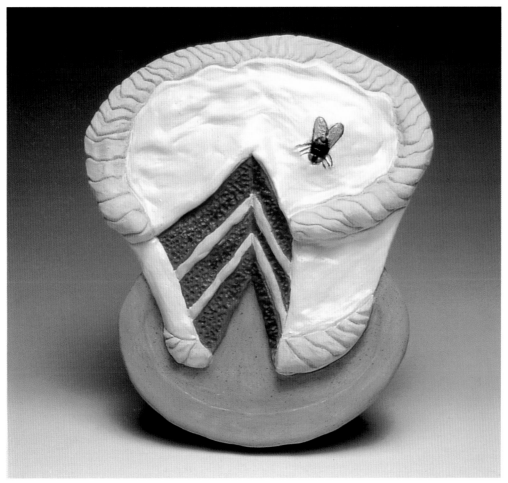

Judith Berk King
Cake & Friend | 2006
10 X 9 X 1 INCHES (25.4 X 22.9 X 2.5 CM)
Earthenware; electric fired,
cone 04; glazed, cone 06
PHOTO BY ARTIST

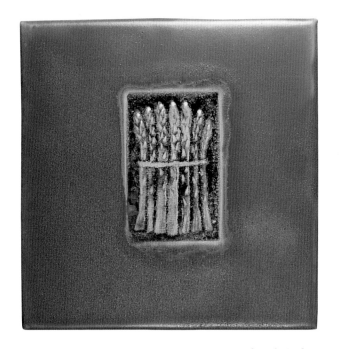

Michael Cohen

Asparagus | 2006

6 X 6 X ¼ INCHES (15.2 X 15.2 X 0.6 CM)

Hand-stamped stoneware tile; gas fired,
cone 9; blue glaze overall, glass

PHOTOS BY ARTIST

Glynnis Condon
John Dory Fossil Plate | 2007
4 1/8 X 9 5/16 X 1/16 INCHES (23.8 X 10.5 X 0.1 CM)
Porcelain slab, stamped with carved cuttle-bone
stamp; cobalt oxide wash; gas fired, oxidation
to vitrification at 2300°F (1260°C)
PHOTO BY ARTIST

Jessica Gorlin Liddell

Morning Cup | 2007

10 X 10 X ½ INCHES (25.4 X 25.4 X 1.3 CM)

Handmade low-fire mosaic; electric
fired, cone 04; glazed, cone 06

PHOTO BY ARTIST

Amanda Jaffe

Gentle Waves II | 2006

8 X 7 X 1½ INCHES (20.3 X 17.8 X 3.8 CM)

Carved porcelain; flowers glazed
to surface; underglaze and glaze;
single-fired in electric kiln, cone 5

PHOTOS BY ARTIST

Melody Ellis

Mr. Punch and His Dog Toby | 2006

11 1/2 X 10 X 1 1/2 INCHES (29.2 X 25.4 X 3.8 CM)

Hand-carved earthenware; slips and underglazes, cone 04; glazes, cone 05

PHOTO BY ARTIST

Bryan Hiveley
The Devil and the Swordfish | 2007
11 X 15 X 1 1/2 INCHES (27.9 X 38.1 X 3.8 CM)
Slab-built and carved stoneware;
oil patina; oxidation fired, cone 04
PHOTO BY ARTIST

Marilyn Sullivan

Vigil | 2006

5 X 6 X 1 ½ INCHES (12.7 X 15.2 X 3.8 CM)

Hand-built earthenware; underglazes
and wash; electric fired, cone 04

PHOTO BY JOHN COYLE

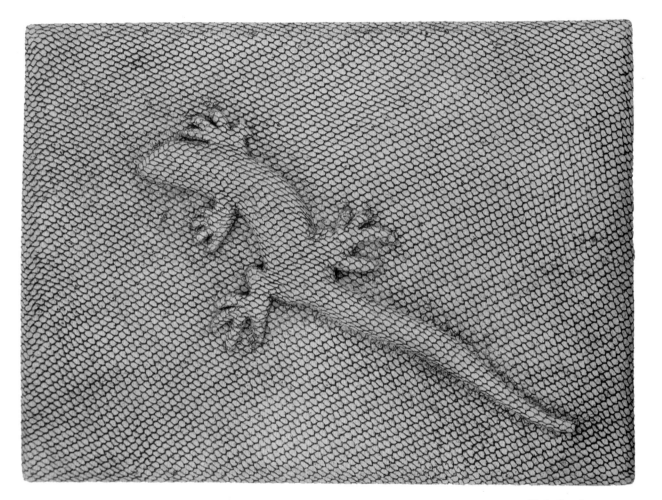

Kristin Antonsen
Salamander | 2007
6¹/₄ X 4¹/₂ X ³/₈ INCHES (15.9 X 11.5 X 1 CM)
Slab-built and textured white stoneware;
electric fired, cone 06; oxides, cone 6
PHOTO BY JOHN ERIK KRISTENSEN

Susan Beiner

Encrusted Field | 2003

112 X 112 X 8 INCHES (284.5 X 284.5 X 20.3 CM)

Slip-cast and assembled
porcelain; gas fired, cone 6

PHOTOS BY SUSAN EINSTEIN

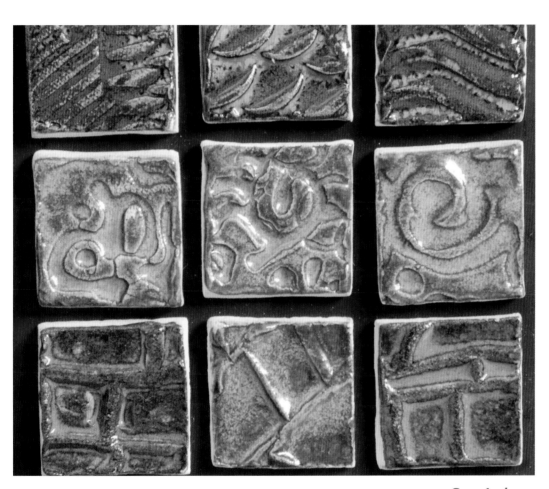

Gary Jackson

ClayQuilt: Slice of Nature | 2006

72 X 6 X 1 INCHES (180 X 15.2 X 2.5 CM)

Textured stoneware tiles;
glazed; fired, cone 6

PHOTOS BY GUY NICOL

Lana Wilson

Almost A Dozen Hands | 2002

12 X 9 X 1½ INCHES (30.5 X 22.9 X 3.8 CM)

Stamped white stoneware; electric fired, glaze firings cones 6 and 04

PHOTO BY ARTIST

Kurt Brian Webb
Death of Corinthian Orders
(Ceramic Toy Theatre
Proscenium) | 2005
15 X 10 X 1 INCHES (38.1 X 25.4 X 2.5 CM)
Carved stoneware; woodfired with soda

PHOTO BY ARTIST

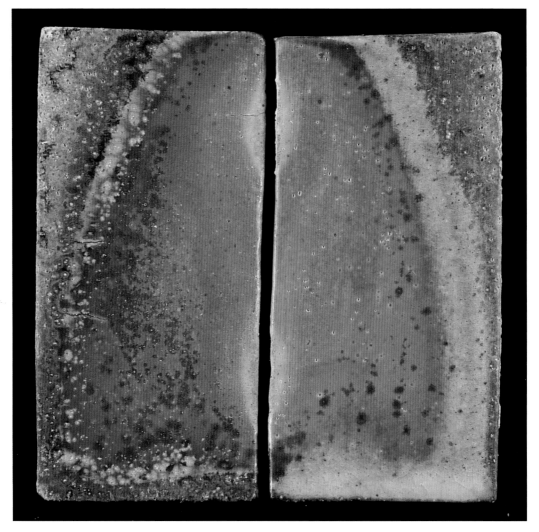

Darren L. Cockrell

Shower Tiles | 2006

EACH: 6 X 3 X ³/₄ INCHES (15.2 X 7.6 X 1.9 CM)

Slab-rolled and hand-cut stoneware;
wood-fired, natural ash glaze, cone 12

PHOTO BY DONALD J. FELTON

Marion Benedek
Bathroom Installation | 2004
5¼ X 5¼ X ⅞ INCHES (13.3 X 13.3 X 2.2 CM)
Press-molded stoneware; electric fired, cone
06; reduction glazed, temmoku, cone 11
PHOTOS BY D. JAMES DEE

Gary Warkentin

Torrey Pine | 2007

6 X 9 X ½ INCHES (15.2 X 22.9 X 1.3 CM)

Press-molded earthenware; electric
fired, cone 04; glazed, cone 06

PHOTO BY ARTIST

Laura McCaul
Two Blackbirds in Reeds | 2007
6 X 8 1/2 X 3/8 INCHES (15.2 X 21.6 X 1 CM)
Hand-pressed red earthenware;
terra sigillata; electric fired, cone
06; wood fired in barrel kiln
PHOTO BY ARTIST

Bryan Hiveley

Dr. Little Kitty Battles the Serpent | 2007

11 X 11 X 1 ¹/₂ INCHES (27.9 X 27.9 X 3.8 CM)

Slab-built and carved stoneware; oil
patina; oxidation fired, cone 04

PHOTO BY ARTIST

Melanie Ann Wegner

Border Tiles - Crows | 2004

24 X 4 INCHES (61 X 10.2 CM)

Press-molded earthenware;
glazed; electric fired, cone 04

PHOTO BY MARGOT GEIST

Christine Emmick

Dragonflys | 2003

8 X 8 INCHES (20.3 X 20.3 CM)

Press-molded raku clay; electric
fired bisque, cone 06; raku glazed,
fired to 1850°F (1010°C)

PHOTO BY ROBERT VIGILETTI

Julie Peck
Rebecca's Story Garden | 2006
33 X 45 X 3 INCHES (83.8 X 114.3 X 7.6 CM)
Earthenware; electric fired, cone 02
PHOTOS BY DEAN POWELL

Barbara Delaney Keirn
…in a Pear Tree | 2006

4 X 4 X ⁷/₈ INCHES (10.2 X 10.2 X 2.2 CM)

Press-molded stoneware; electric
fired, cone 04; bisque fired, underglaze, cone 04; glaze, cone 5

PHOTO BY SLIDE SERVICE INTERNATIONAL

Michael Cohen
Tree | 2006
6 X 6 X ¼ INCHES (15.2 X 15.2 X 0.6 CM)
Hand-stamped stoneware tile; gas fired,
cone 9; blue glaze overall, glass
PHOTOS BY ARTIST

Dawn Detarando
Fox & Raven | 2000
6 X 6 X ³⁄₈ INCHES (15.2 X 15.2 X 1 CM)
Hand-pressed terra cotta;
electric fired, cone 04; glaze
PHOTO BY ARTIST

Carrie Anne Parks

Green Tiles | 2002

15³/₈ X 13¹/₈ X 2 INCHES (39.1 X 33.3 X 5.1 CM)

Press-molded earthenware; electric fired,
cone 06; underglazed, cone 05

PHOTO BY ARTIST

Earline M. Green
*Fulfilling the Dream; Along District Lines
(Roosevelt High School Spirit Quilt)* | 2006

72 X 54 X 4 INCHES (182.9 X 137.2 X 10.2 CM)

Press-molded stoneware; bisque fired, cone 1;
underglazed and glazed, cone 06; electric kiln

PHOTOS BY HARRISON EVANS

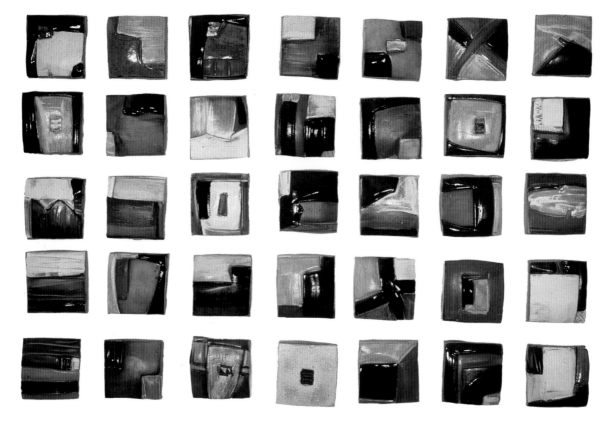

Ellen Huie
Boston Grid (detail on facing page) | 2007
28 X 20 X 1 1/2 INCHES (71.1 X 50.8 X 3.8 CM)
Earthenware; electric fired, cone 04
PHOTOS BY LARRY GAWEL

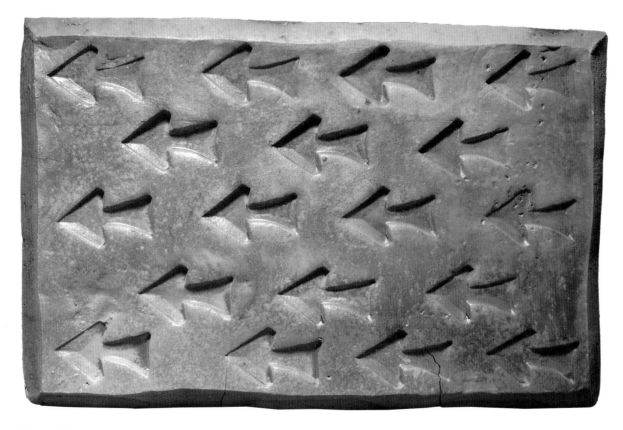

Matt Moyer

This Way | 2005

20 X 12 X 2 INCHES (50.8 X 30.5 X 5.1 CM)

Stoneware; wood-fired, cone 10, natural ash

PHOTO BY ARTIST

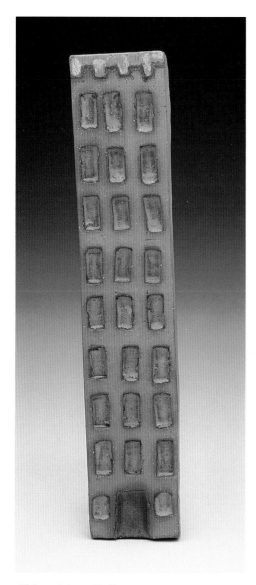

Chloë Marr-Fuller
Tall Building | 2006
5¹/₂ X 1 X ¹/₄ INCHES (14 X 2.5 X 0.6 CM)
Slab-rolled terra cotta; electric
fired, cone 04; carved, glazed
PHOTO BY MONICA RIPLEY

Marianne Kokkoros
Ceramic Tiles Wall Hanging | 2006
38 X 15 INCHES (96.5 X 38.1 CM)
Stoneware; electric fired, cone 6;
underglazes and oxides
PHOTO BY GREGORY R. STALEY

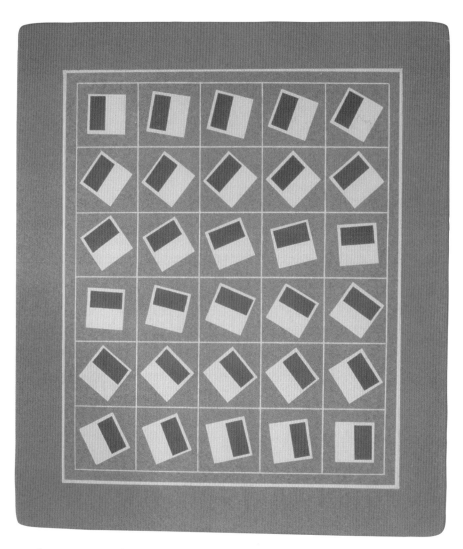

Andrew VanAssche

Rotation | 2006

11 1/4 X 10 X 3/8 INCHES (28.6 X 25.4 X 1 CM)

Slab-rolled stoneware; oxidation fired,
cone 4; clay slips decoration

PHOTO BY ARTIST

Janey Skeer
Blue Window | 2006
19 X 9 X 1 1/2 INCHES (48.3 X 22.9 X 3.8 CM)
Hand-built; terra sigillata and stain surface
work, stamped impressions; cone 04,
bisque; electric fired, cone 3
PHOTO BY CHARLIE ROY

Gary Warkentin
Bald Cypress with Moon | 2005
10 X 5 X 1/2 INCHES (25.4 X 12.7 X 1.3 CM)
Press-molded earthenware; electric
fired, cone 04; glazed, cone 06
PHOTO BY COURTNEY FRISSE

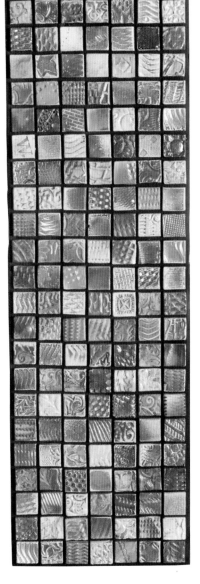

Gary Jackson

ClayQuilt: Tones & Textures | 2006

36 X 12 X 1 INCHES (91.4 X 30.5 X 2.5 CM)

Textured stoneware, slip painted; soda-fired, cone 10

PHOTOS BY GUY NICOL

Nancy Chevalier Guido
Large Architectural Tile | 2002
10 X 10 X ½ INCHES (25.4 X 25.4 X 1.3 CM)
Press-molded terra cotta;
multi-fired in electric kiln, cone 6;
layered stains and engobes
PHOTO BY BRIAN GUIDO

Jane McFarland Garrett

Three Hares | 2006

4¹⁄₄ X 4¹⁄₄ X ³⁄₈ INCHES (10.8 X 10.8 X 1 CM)

Press-molded white stoneware; electric
fired, cone 05; glazed and wiped, cone 6

PHOTO BY ARTIST

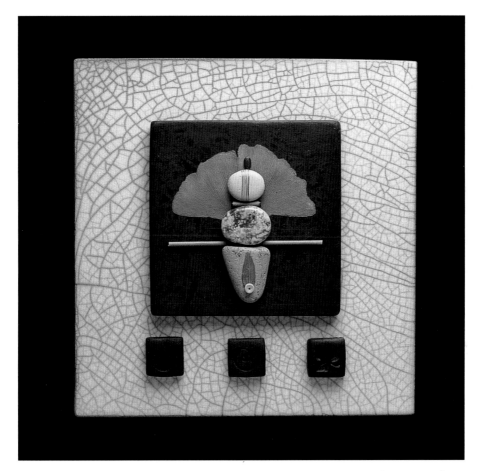

Steve Vachon
Sue Davis-Vachon

Ginkgo Tile Assemblage | 2006

8 X 8 X ½ INCHES (20.3 X 20.3 X 1.3 CM)

Hand-cut stoneware, spray glazed; raku fired,
cone 09; assembled post-firing, found objects

PHOTO BY ARTIST

Lisa Muller

House Portrait Tile | 2006

8 X 5⁵/₁₆ X 1¹/₂ INCHES (20.3 X 13.5 X 3.8 CM)

Hand-built and carved earthenware;
sprigged; electric fired, cone 1;
glaze fired, cone 03

PHOTO BY JAY WILEY

Lana Wilson

Hand and Buddha | 2002

9 X 5 X 2½ INCHES (22.9 X 12.7 X 6.4 CM)

Stamped white stoneware; bamboo,
cones, colored cement, wood; electric
fired, glaze firings, cones 6 and 04

PHOTO BY ARTIST

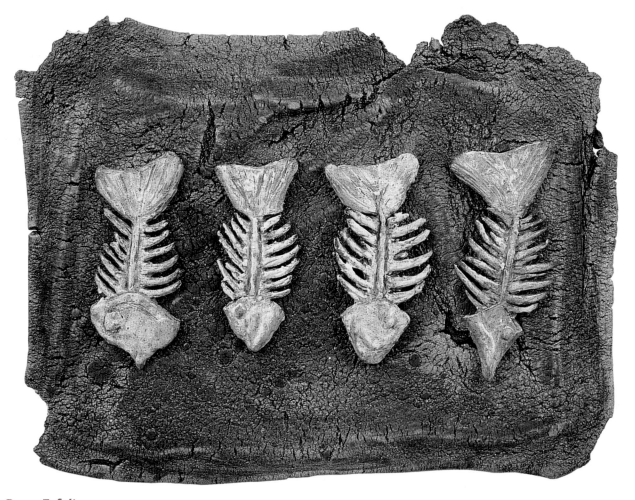

Rena Fafalios

Aegean Frieze | 2007

8³⁄₄ X 12¹⁄₄ X ³⁄₄ INCHES (22.2 X 31.1 X 1.9 CM)

Stoneware, slips; electric fired, cone 6; acrylics

PHOTO BY D. JAMES DEE

Novie Trump

Goldfinch | 2006

9 X 7 X 1 INCHES (22.9 X 17.8 X 2.5 CM)

Mid-range, outdoor sculpture body clay;
electric fired, cone 06; glazed with
Mason stains, oxides, and slips, cone 6

PHOTO BY GREG STALEY

Elizabeth A. Vorlicek

Finger Printed Tile Box | 2002

9¹/₂ X 7¹/₂ X 2¹/₂ INCHES (24.1 X 19.1 X 6.4 CM)

Slab-built stoneware; electric
fired, cone 04; multi-fired

PHOTO BY ARTIST

Marilyn Dennis Palsha
Pole Dancer Tile | 2007
9 1/2 X 6 X 3/8 INCHES (24.1 X 15.2 X 1 CM)
Slab-built red earthenware; electric
fired, cone 03; maiolica glaze, painted
stains, glazed fired, cone 02
PHOTO BY SETH TICE-LEWIS

Rimas VisGirda

Women with Balls | 2006

10 X 11 X 1 ½ INCHES (25.4 X 27.9 X 3.8 CM)

Slab-rolled porcelain with decomposed granite;
natural edges, slip-trailed drawing; electric fired,
cone 10; lusters, overglazes, and decals, cone 017

PHOTO BY ARTIST

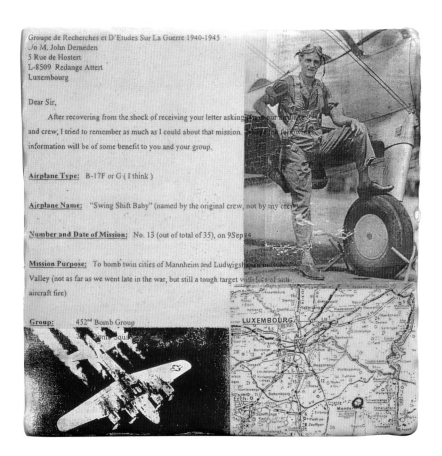

Maggie Mae Beyeler

The 13th Mission of Swing Shift Baby | 2007

EACH: 8 X 8 X 5/16 INCHES (20.3 X 20.3 X 0.8 CM)

Slab-rolled white stoneware; electric fired, cone 6; laser toner image transfer, cone 04

PHOTOS BY MARGOT GEIST

Brenda B. Townsend
Abstract Kimono 12 | 2004
28 X 16 INCHES (71.1 X 40.6 CM)
Cut; handmade glazes; raku fired
PHOTO BY CHIP FEISE LOCATION PHOTOGRAPHY

Sara Behling
Healing Wound | 2005
4 X 3 X ¹/₁₆ INCHES (10.2 X 7.6 X 0.2 CM)
Translucent porcelain; cone 10, luster glazes
PHOTO BY CHARLIE ROY

JoAnn Aquinto
Florentine Tile | 2006
11 X 12 X 1 INCHES (27.9 X 30.5 X 2.5 CM)
Press-molded stoneware; electric
fired, cone 6; inlaid glazes
PHOTO BY ARTIST

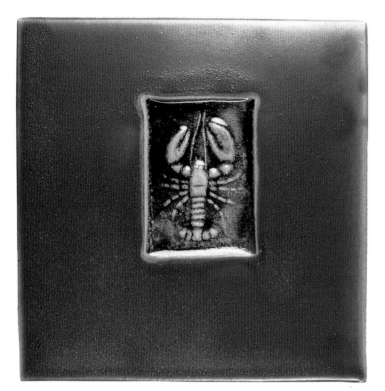

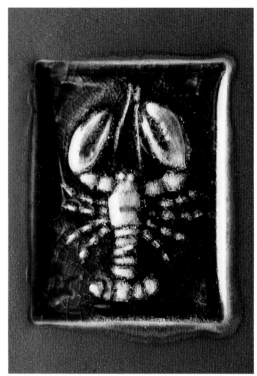

Michael Cohen
Lobster | 2006
6 X 6 X ¼ INCHES (15.2 X 15.2 X 0.6 CM)
Hand-stamped stoneware tile; gas fired,
cone 9; blue glaze overall, glass
PHOTOS BY ARTIST

Valerie Nicklow
Jonathan Nicklow

Allure of a Life Worth Living | 2006

16 X 12 X ½ INCHES (40.6 X 30.5 X 1.3 CM)

Low-fire white clay; electric fired,
cone 04; slab-rolled, relief
sculpture, oil paints and varnish

PHOTO BY ARTIST

Jenny Mendes
One Heart | 2006
11 X 8 1/2 X 1/4 INCHES (27.9 X 21.6 X 0.6 CM)
Hand-rolled earthenware slab; terra sigillata
with sgraffito; electric fired, cone 03
PHOTO BY TOM MILLS

Jane McFarland Garrett
Tree Hugger | 2006
4 1/4 X 4 1/4 X 1/4 INCHES (10.8 X 10.8 X 0.6 CM)
Press-molded white stoneware; electric
fired, cone 05; glazed and wiped, cone 6
PHOTO BY ARTIST

Sarah Raymond
Ornamental Popsicles | 2007
5⁷/₈ X 5⁷/₈ X 1³/₁₆ INCHES (15 X 15 X 3 CM)
Hand-built stoneware; double-walled
construction; underglaze painted with
sgraffito drawing; electric fired, cone 6
PHOTO BY VINCE NOGUCHI

JoAnn Aquinto

Tile Panel | 1995

12 X 12 X ⅝ INCHES (30.5 X 30.5 X 1.6 CM)

Press-molded stoneware; electric
fired, inlaid glazes, cone 6

PHOTO BY ARTIST

Kimberly Rorick
Red Tea Pot Relief Tile | 2005
13 1/2 X 13 1/2 INCHES (34.3 X 34.3 CM)
Porcelain; slab-rolled relief; underglaze
and glaze; electric fired, cone 6
PHOTOS BY ACCU COLOR

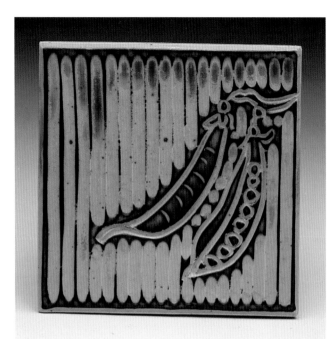

Gabrielle Fougere

Peas | 2006

3 1/2 X 3 1/2 X 1/4 INCHES (8.9 X 8.9 X 0.6 CM)

Slab-rolled stoneware with black slip;
gas fired in reduction, cone 10

PHOTO BY MONICA RIPLEY

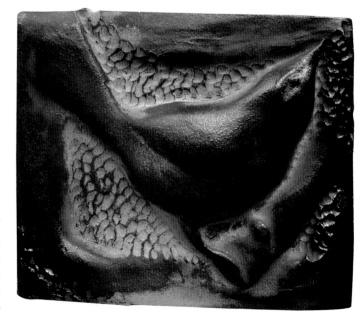

Keri Huber

Catbird | 2005

2 3/4 X 3 1/4 X 1/2 INCHES (7 X 8.9 X 1.3 CM)

Press-molded earthenware, altered; bisque
fired, cone 04; stain; sodafired, cone 04

PHOTO BY JERRY MATHIASONL

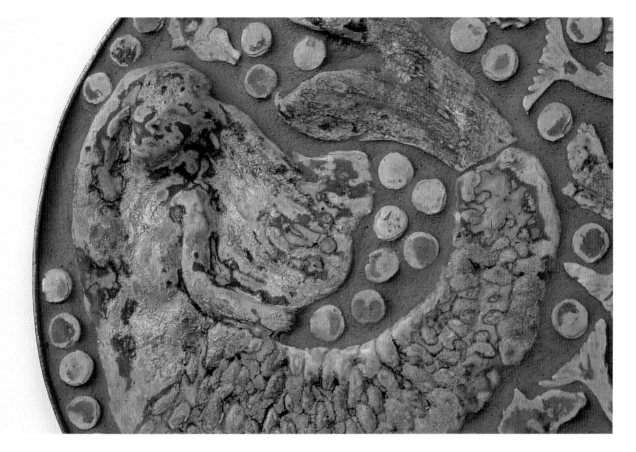

Jan Suarez
Ship-Wrecked Mermaid | 2006
14 X ½ INCHES (35.6 X 1.3 CM)
Hand-cut stoneware; electric fired,
bisque cone 06; glazed, cone 5
PHOTOS BY MARTHA LOCHERT PHOTOGRAPHY

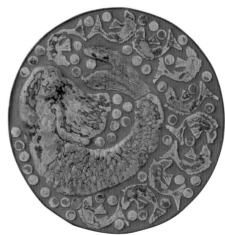

Marilyn Dennis Palsha
Mermaid Tile | 2007
7 X ³/₈ INCHES (17.8 X 1 CM)
Slab-built red earthenware; electric
fired, cone 03; maiolica glaze,
painted stains, glazed fired, cone 02
PHOTO BY SETH TICE-LEWIS

"Do not take life's experiences too seriously. Above all, do not let them hurt you, for in reality they are nothing but dream experiences. Play your part in life, but never forget it is only a role."

Yogananda

Nan Smith

In Sight | 1994

22³/₄ X 33¹/₂ X 1¹/₂ INCHES (57.8 X 85.1 X 3.8 CM)

Tamped and rolled buff earthenware; bisque, electric fired, cone 03; airbrushed and brushed underglaze applied to bisque; glaze, cone 04; color graduated with airbrushed bisque stains

PHOTOS BY ALLEN CHEUVRONT

Richard Notkin

All Nations Have Their Moment of Foolishness | 2007

46 X 60¼ X 4½ INCHES (116.8 X 153 X 11.4 CM)

Press-molded earthenware; gasfired in sawdust-filled saggars,
cone 04; unglazed; post-fired watercolor highlights

PHOTO BY ARTIST

Frances Norton
Visitation | 1992
7⅞ X 7⅞ X ⅜ INCHES (20 X 20 X 1 CM)
Terra cotta; white slip and oxides;
electric fired, 1940°F (1060°C)
PHOTO BY ARTIST

Valerie Nicklow
Jonathan Nicklow
Otis Orvis | 2005
16 X 12 X ½ INCHES (40.6 X 30.5 X 1.3 CM)
Low-fire white clay; electric fired,
cone 04; slab-rolled, relief sculpture,
oil paints and varnish
PHOTO BY ARTIST

Anne Lloyd
Black Lab | 2001
8 X 6 INCHES (20.3 X 15.2 CM)
Raku; bas-relief; low-fire,
cone 6; glazes
PHOTO BY JOHN CARLANO

Jeanie B. Daves
*Guatemalan Grandmother
and Child* | 2006
18 X 14 X 1 1/2 INCHES (45.7 X 35.6 X 3.8 CM)
Hand-built earthenware; electric
fired, cone 02; copper carbonate
wash, cone 04; acrylic sealer

PHOTO BY ARTIST

Keri Huber

Bluebird | 2004

4 X 5¼ X ½ INCHES (10.2 X 13.3 X 1.3 CM)

Hand-built earthenware; bisque fired,
cone 04; terra sigillata, pitfired

PHOTO BY JERRY MATHIASON

Irina Clopatofsky Velasco
Prairie Bison | 2006
6¹/₂ X 6¹/₂ X ¹/₄ INCHES (15.9 X 15.9 X 0.6 CM)
Pressed stoneware; glass,
oxides; electric fired, cone 6
PHOTO BY ERIC KANE

Laurie Eisenhardt

The Queen and King | 2005

EACH: 6 X 6 INCHES (15.2 X 15.2 CM)

Press-molded, low-fire clay body;
underglazes and glazes

PHOTO BY RICHARD DOYLE

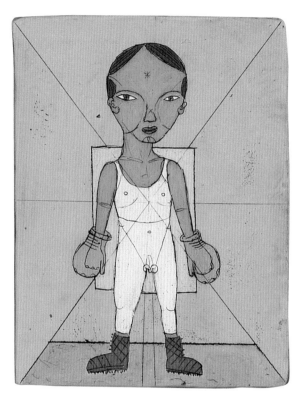

Jenny Mendes
Live Free or Die | 2005
EACH: 5 X 3½ X ¼ INCHES (12.7 X 8.9 X 0.6 CM)
Hand-rolled earthenware slab; terra sigillata
with sgraffito; electric fired, cone 03
PHOTO BY TOM MILLS

Elaine Bolz

Emergence | 2003

16 X 24 X 2 INCHES (40.6 X 61 X 5.1 CM)

White earthenware clay; electric fired,
cone 02; multi-fired, cone 05; airbrushed
and painted with underglazes

PHOTO BY ARTIST

Pat Johnson
Hildegard | 2000
72 X 48 INCHES (182.9 X 121.9 CM)
Bisque commercial Dal-Tile; electric
fired, underglazed and glazed, cone 06
PHOTOS BY HESTER+HARDAWAY PHOTOGRAPHY

Skuja Braden

Guan Yin | 2005

EACH: 6 X 6 INCHES (15.2 X 15.2 CM)

Hand-pressed porcelain tiles; electric fired,
cone 4; inscribed designs, glazes, stains, cone 6

PHOTOS BY TONY NOVOLOZO

Susan Beiner
Garden Tile Block | 1999
7 X 10 X 6 INCHES (17.8 X 25.4 X 15.2 CM)
Slip-cast and assembled
porcelain; salt-fired, cone 10
PHOTO BY TIM THAYER

Diana Watson

Mujedar Fountain | 2005

54 X 30 INCHES (137.2 X 76.2 CM)

Ram press-molded terra cotta; electric fired, cone 05; silkscreened pattern outline; hand-glazed custom glazes

PHOTOS BY EDMUND BARR

Susan Siegele
Bathroom Counter 1 | 1998
9 X 37 X 22 INCHES (22.9 X 94 X 55.9 CM)
Inlaid colored porcelain; wood fired, cone 10

PHOTO BY MIKE HALEY

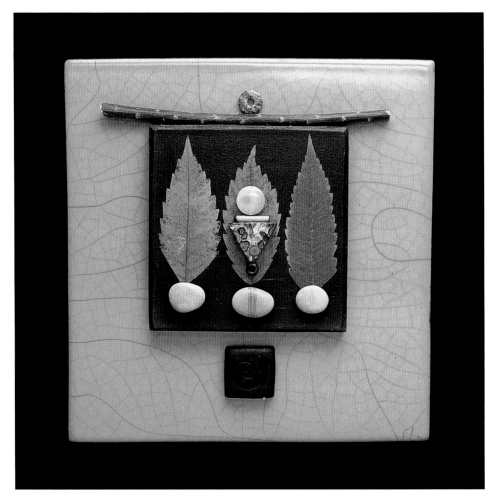

Steve Vachon
Sue Davis-Vachon

Sumac Tile Assemblage | 2006

8 X 8 X ½ INCHES (20.3 X 20.3 X 1.3 CM)

Hand-cut stoneware, spray glazed; raku fired,
cone 09; assembled post-firing, found objects

Nicholas Wood
Sampler - Europa # 10 | 2003
68 X 125 X 2¹/₂ INCHES (172.7 X 317.5 X 6.4 CM)
Multiple cast raw clays; stains,
colorants, resins, wood

PHOTOS BY ARTIST

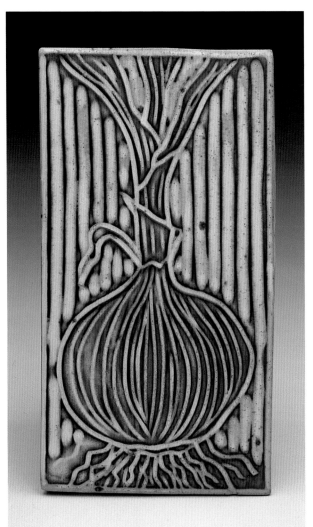

Gabrielle Fougere
Onion | 2006

5 1/4 X 3 X 1/4 INCHES (13.3 X 7.6 X 0.6 CM)

Slab-rolled stoneware with black slip;
gas fired in reduction, cone 10

PHOTO BY MONICA RIPLEY

Irina Clopatofsky Velasco
Chartres Labyrinth | 2006

7 3/8 X 7 1/2 X 1/2 INCHES (18.8 X 19.1 X 1.3 CM)

Hand-pressed stoneware, partially
glazed; electric fired, cone 6

PHOTO BY ERIC KANE

David Ellison
Floral Plaque | 2006
13 X 18 X 1 ¼ INCHES (33 X 45.7 X 3.2 CM)
Press-molded terra cotta; oxidized, cone 04
PHOTO BY PATRICK YOUNG

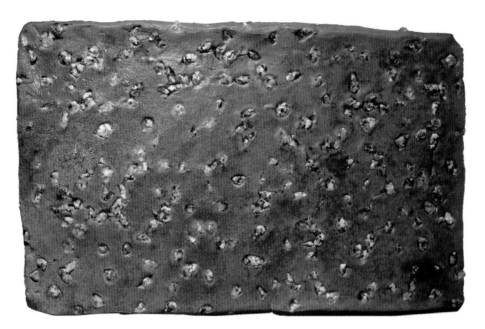

Matt Moyer

Untitled 2 | 2005

20 X 12 X 2 INCHES (50.8 X 30.5 X 5.1 CM)

Stoneware; wood-fired, cone 10, natural ash

PHOTO BY ARTIST

Sheldon Ganstrom

Razor Dance | 2006

11 X 11 ½ X ½ INCHES (27.9 X 29.2 X 1.3 CM)

Slab-rolled stoneware clay with 15-percent
Kyanite; bisque fired, cone 08; electric fired
with post-fired reduction techniques, cone 07

PHOTO BY ARTIST

Rebeca D. Gilling
Rosemary | 2006
11 X 13 X 1/2 INCHES (27.9 X 33 X 1.3 CM)
Hand-built; electric fired; glazed
PHOTO BY J. KING

Barbara Delaney Keirn
Horse of a Different Color | 2006
4 X 4 X ¾ INCHES (10.2 X 10.2 X 1.9 CM)
Press-molded stoneware; electric fired, cone 04;
bisque fired, cone 5; commercial blue rutile glaze
PHOTO BY SLIDE SERVICE INTERNATIONAL

Lois Kay Peterson
Listening at the Edge Series Tile #1 | 2003
13 X 13 X 3 INCHES (33 X 33 X 7.6 CM)
Press-molded stoneware; electric fired,
cone 04; commercial iron finish
PHOTO BY NELL YTSMA

Lynn Smiser Bowers

3 Sunflowers | 2007

8 X 8 X ¼ INCHES (20.3 X 20.3 X 0.6 CM)

Hand-cut porcelain slab; wax resist, oxides, stencils; gas fired in reduction, cone 10

PHOTO BY MARCUS SKALA

Janey Skeer

Green Door | 2006

19 X 9 X 1½ INCHES (48.3 X 22.9 X 3.8 CM)

Hand-built; terra sigillata and stain surface work, stamped impressions; cone 04, bisque; electric fired, cone 3

PHOTO BY CHARLIE ROY

Steve Howell
Sun and Moon | 2006

16 X 16 INCHES (40.6 X 40.6 CM)

Slab-built red earthenware; electric fired,
glazed, cone 06; gold luster, cone 010

PHOTO BY RANDALL SMITH

Hennie Meyer

Fragments | 2006

EACH: 2³/₄ X 2³/₄ X 2³/₄ INCHES (7 X 7 X 7 CM)

Slab-built earthenware, painted slip;
glaze, oxides; electric fired, cone 2

PHOTO BY ARTIST

Jonathan Nicklow
Butterfly and Flowers | 2006
8 X 8 X ¾ INCHES (20.3 X 20.3 X 1.9 CM)
Low-fire white clay; electric fired, cone
04; slab-rolled, relief sculpture, stamped
elements, oil paint, and varnish
PHOTO BY ARTIST

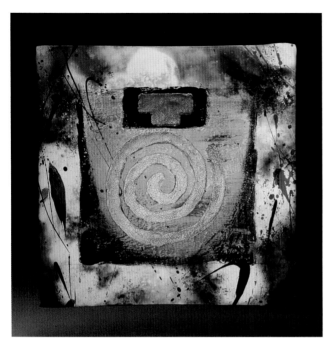

Steve Howell

Shield | 2006

16 X 16 INCHES (40.6 X 40.6 CM)

Porcelain slab; electric fired, glaze fired, cone 07; gold luster fired, cone 010; pit fired

PHOTO BY RANDALL SMITH

Lana Wilson

Layered Tiles | 2007

6 X 6 X 1 INCHES (15.2 X 15.2 X 2.5 CM)

Textured white stoneware; electric fired, cone 6

PHOTO BY ARTIST

Jennifer A. Everett
Tile | 2006
3 X 3 X ³/₈ INCHES (7.6 X 7.6 X 1 CM)
Extruded stoneware with stamped
decoration; gas fired in reduction, cone 10

PHOTO BY ARTIST

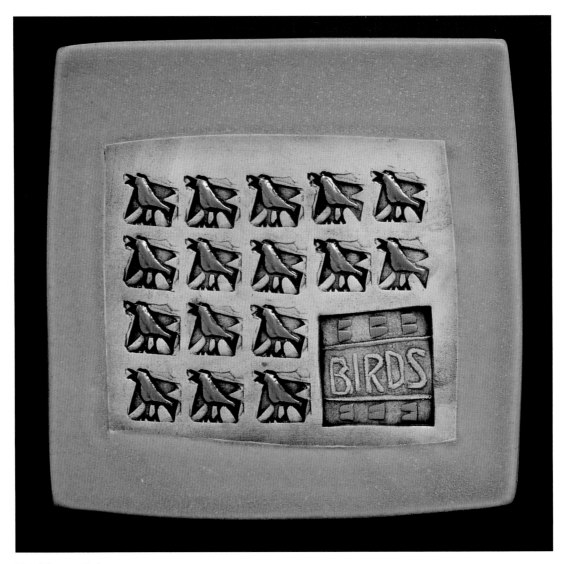

Kathleen Koltes

Birds | 2007

6 X 6 X 3/8 INCHES (15.2 X 15.2 X 1 CM)

Slab-rolled stoneware; hand-carved stamps;
underglazes; electric glaze-fired, cone 6

PHOTO BY MARGOT GEIST

Melody Ellis

Pants Tile and Greyhound Tile | 2003

EACH: 5 X 5 X ½ INCHES (12.7 X 12.7 X 1.3 CM)

Hand-carved earthenware; electric
fired, cone 04; black grout

PHOTO BY ARTIST

Lauren Lewis

Path | 2005

22 X 24 X 1½ INCHES (55.9 X 61 X 3.8 CM)

Slab- and hand-built earthenware; electric
fired, cone 04; oxide wash, cone 04

PHOTO BY STEVE MANN

Jan Robb

Bleeding Hearts | 2006

8 X 4 X ½ INCHES (20.3 X 10.2 X 1.3 CM)

Press-molded porcelain;
electric fired, cone 5

PHOTO BY MARK TRUPIANO

Melody Cooper

Requiescat for Steve | 2005

5¼ X 5¼ INCHES (13.3 X 13.3 CM)

Hand-carved stoneware; downdraft gas
kiln, cone 10; Lung-ch'uan celadon glaze

PHOTO BY TONY CUNHA

Elizabeth Smith Jacobs

The Unity Wall Project | 2006

564 X 35 X 3 INCHES (1432.6 X 88.9 X 7.6 CM);
EACH TILE: 4 X 4 INCHES (10.2 X 10.2 CM)

Hand-built bas-relief porcelain; electric fired,
cone 6; underglazes with cone 6 clear glaze

PHOTOS BY PETER JACOBS FINE ART PHOTOGRAPHY

Dalia Laučkaité-Jakimavičiené

Vista Panoramica | 2006

13 X 98¼ X ⅜ INCHES (33 X 250 X 1 CM)

Manufactured tiles, glazes, laser print
decals; cone 07, onglaze decals, china
paints, gold, platinum lusters; cone 016

PHOTO BY VIDMANTAS ILLČIUKAS

Ivy Glasgow

Opal Blue Buttons, Modern Series | 2007

EACH: 41/2 X 41/2 X 1/2 INCHES (11.4 X 11.4 X 1.3 CM)

Press-molded and altered stoneware; fired, cone 6

PHOTO BY ARTIST

Andrew VanAssche
Lyric | 2006
11 ¼ X 10 X ⅜ INCHES (28.6 X 25.4 X 1 CM)
Slab-rolled stoneware; oxidation
fired, cone 4; clay slips decoration
PHOTO BY ARTIST

Janet Fergus
Monkey Fountain Panel | 2004
18 X 12 X ³⁄₈ INCHES (45.7 X 30.5 X 1 CM)
Press-molded earthenware; electric fired, cone 05; hand-painted with commercial low-fire glazes
PHOTO BY ELIZABETH ELLINGSON

Mary Philpott
Art Nouveau Poppy Art Tile | 2006
12 X 6 INCHES (30.5 X 15.2 CM)
Hand-carved, -pressed, and glazed porcelain; electric fired, multi-fired, cone 7
PHOTO BY ARTIST

Bonnie J. Smith
Texture and Equality #1 | 2006
12 X 12 INCHES (30.5 X 30.5 CM)
Slab-rolled and textured earthenware tiles; electric fired,
cone 05; glazed; raku fired to 1850°F (1010°C); newspaper
reduction; assembled and affixed to black stained MDF

PHOTO BY DAVID WILDER

Norma Hanlon
Kirsten Walstead
Tree of Life Tile Mural | 2005
21 X 21 X 2½ INCHES (53.3 X 53.3 X 6.4 CM)
Press-molded stoneware; electric fired, cone 4
PHOTO BY DIGIGRAPHICS

Justin Rothshank
Wall Tile #1 | 2005
14 X 14 X 5 INCHES (35.6 X 35.6 X 12.7 CM)
Wheel-thrown and altered stoneware; reduction
fired, cone 10; shino glaze, pinewood frame
PHOTO BY DAVID L. SMITH

Tiffany Schmierer

The Swan | 2006

16 X 19 X 5 INCHES (40.6 X 48.3 X 12.7 CM)

Hand-built earthenware; electric fired,
cone 04; underglaze and glaze firing,
cone 06 and 07; luster firing, cone 019

Shay Amber
Perch 2 | 2006
9 X 9 X 2 INCHES (22.9 X 22.9 X 5.1 CM)
Stiff-slab construction; multi-fired, cone 016, decal
PHOTO BY STEVE MANN

Hwang Jeng-daw
Mechanical Time | 2004
79 X 118 X 4 INCHES (200 X 300 X 10 CM)
Slab-built stoneware; gas
fired, glazed, cone 9; gold
and platinum luster, cone 012

PHOTO BY ARTIST

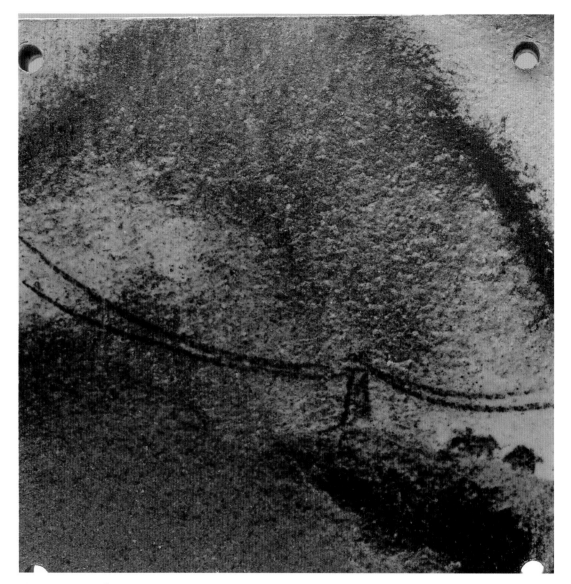

Hwang Jeng-daw

Norwegian Mountain Landscape No. 1 | 2002

3 15/16 X 3 15/16 X 3/8 INCHES (10 X 10 X 1 CM)

Slab-built porcelain, mixed colored
clay; electric fired, cone 9

PHOTO BY ARTIST

Kristen Kieffer
Fat Tiles | 2006
EACH: 4^1/$_2$ X 4^1/$_2$ X 1^3/$_4$ INCHES (11.4 X 11.4 X 4.4 CM)
Hand-built, stamped, and slipped white stoneware;
glazed; soda-fired in reduction, cone 10

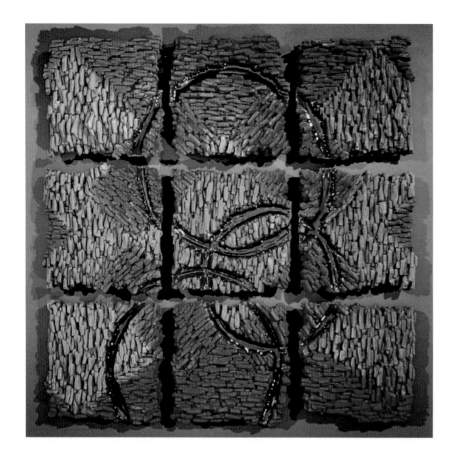

Michael Allen Gregory
Displaced Purple Square | 2006
30 X 30 X 2 INCHES (76.2 X 76.2 X 5.1 CM)
Press-molded sculpture clay; electric fired,
cone 1; multi-fired washes and frit, cone 03
PHOTOS BY EDDIE ING

Elizabeth A. Vorlicek
Merge | 2002
180 X 180 X 3 INCHES (457.2 X 457.2 X 7.6 CM)
Slab-built, press-molded terra cotta; slips,
Xerox transfer; electric fired, cone 02
PHOTOS BY ARTIST

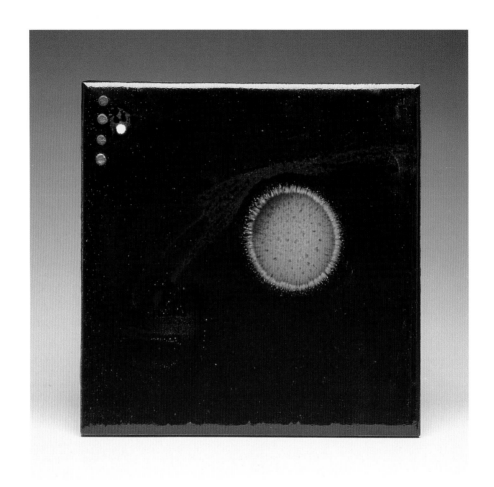

Jonathan Hawkins

Red Dwarf | 2005

6 X 6 X 5/16 INCHES (15.2 X 15.2 X 0.8 CM)

Pressed earthenware; electric fired,
cone 03; glazed, cone 07

PHOTO BY JASON LACHTARA

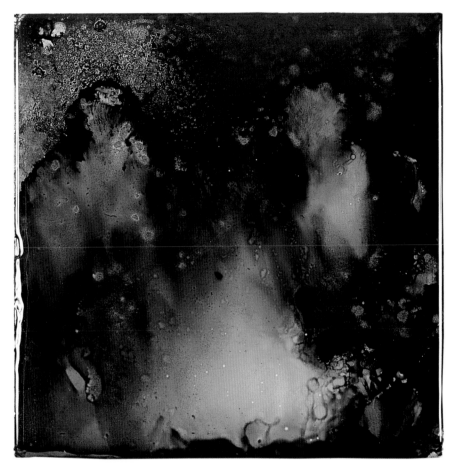

Cynthia Luhrs
Color Series #5 | 2006
6 X 6 INCHES (15.2 X 15.2 CM)
Ceramic; painted with acrylics, inks, and
Pearl Ex powders; glazed; clear resin
PHOTO BY LYNN RUCK

John Heaney

Tile | 2006

9 X 10¹/₄ X ³/₄ INCHES (23 X 26 X 2 CM)

Wire-cut slab; wood fired, salt glaze
over cobalt black slip, cone 13

PHOTO BY STEWART HAY

Novie Trump

Black Birds on Wire Fence | 2006

6 X 9¹/₂ X 1 INCHES (15.2 X 24.1 X 2.5 CM)

Mid-range, outdoor sculpture body clay;
electric fired, cone 06; glazed with
Mason stains, oxides, and slips, cone 6

PHOTO BY GREG STALEY

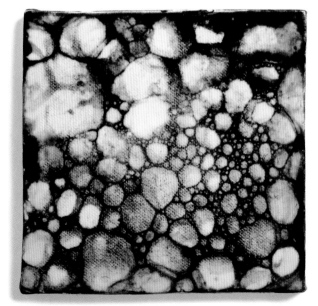

Brooks Bouwkamp

Rocks | 2007

5¹/₄ X 5¹/₄ X ¹/₄ INCHES (13.3 X 13.3 X 0.6 CM)

Hand-built white stoneware; electric fired, cone 10

PHOTO BY DAVE SHERWIN

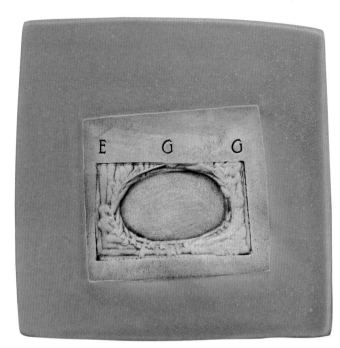

Kathleen Koltes

Egg | 2007

6 X 6 X ⅜ INCHES (15.2 X 15.2 X 1 CM)

Slab-rolled stoneware; hand-carved linoleum
block; metal type; electric glaze-fired, cone 6

PHOTO BY MARGOT GEIST

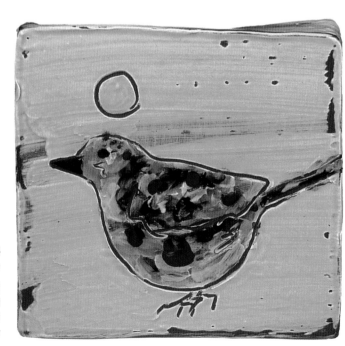

Shaunna Lyons

Break of Day Bird | 2007

4½ X 4¾ X 1 INCHES (11.4 X 12.1 X 2.5 CM)

Slab-built low-fire red clay, slips and fritted
stains; electric fired, cone 03; glazed, cone 05

PHOTO BY WALKER MONTGOMERY

Farraday Newsome
Icarus | 2003
7 X 7 X ³/₄ INCHES (17.8 X 17.8 X 1.9 CM)
Cut terra cotta slab; bisque fired, cone 1;
brushed glazes, electric fired, cone 05
PHOTO BY ARIST

Paul Andrew Wandless
St. Pablo the Fighter | 2007
10 X 13¼ X ½ INCHES (25.4 X 33.7 X 1.3 CM)
Monotype, stamped on white stoneware;
electric fired, cone 04; slips, glaze, cone 04
PHOTO BY ARTIST

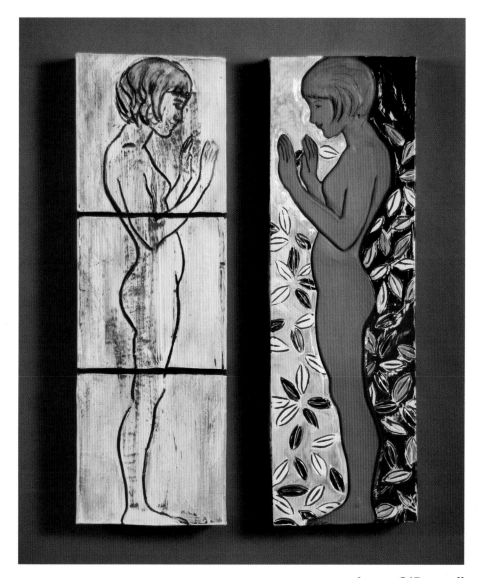

Laura O'Donnell

Spring and Autumn | 2005

EACH: 16³⁄₈ X 6³⁄₈ X 2³⁄₈ INCHES (41.6 X 16.2 X 6.1 CM)

Slab-built and modeled earthenware; white slip,
sgraffito decoration; underglazes, clear glaze,
ceramic stains; electric fired, cone 03

PHOTO BY ARTIST

Valerie Nicklow
Jonathan Nicklow

The Chronologer | 2006

16 X 12 X ½ INCHES (40.6 X 30.5 X 1.3 CM)

Low-fire white clay; electric fired, cone 04; slab-rolled, relief
sculpture, stamped elements with oil paints and varnish

PHOTO BY ARTIST

Jenny Mendes

The Midnight Gardener | 2006
11 X 8½ X ¼ INCHES (27.9 X 21.6 X 0.6 CM)

Hand-rolled earthenware slab; terra sigillata
with sgraffito; electric fired, cone 03

PHOTO BY TOM MILLS

Irina Clopatofsky Velasco

La Jirafa | 2005

8 X 6 X 3/8 INCHES (20.3 X 15.2 X 1 CM)

White stoneware; Helmer slip; shell, unglazed; anagama fired, cone 13

PHOTO BY ERIC KANE

Sarah Fitch
Blue Dragon | 2006
7½ X 10 X ¼ INCHES (19.1 X 25.4 X 0.6 CM)
Hand-carved stoneware relief, porcelain;
electric fired, cone 5; stain and glazes
PHOTO BY FRANK ROSS

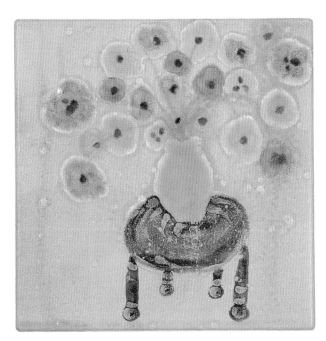

Joan Rothchild Hardin

Flowers in Blue Vase | 2004

6 X 6 X ¼ INCHES (15.2 X 15.2 X 0.6 CM)

Hand-painted commercial bisque tile;
Amaco glazes; electric fired, cone 05

PHOTO BY JAMES DEE

Jan Robb

Plantation #1 | 2006

6 X 6 X ½ INCHES (15.2 X 15.2 X 1.3 CM)

Press-molded porcelain;
electric fired, cone 5

PHOTO BY MARK TRUPIANO

Jen Winfrey
Ode to Georgia's Poppies | 2006
29 X 48 INCHES (73.7 X 121.9 CM)
Slab-rolled white earthenware; electric
fired, cone 05; glazed, cone 05
PHOTO BY ARTIST

Skuja Braden

Flowers | 2005

TALLEST: 180 X 240 INCHES (457.2 X 609.6 CM)

Hand-pressed porcelain tiles; inscribed designs, glazes, and stains; electric fired, cone 6

PHOTOS BY MELISSA BRADEN

**Lynn Render
Ann Hobart
Pat McGregor**

Spanish Village Art Center, Fountain | 2004

96 X 96 INCHES (243.8 X 243.8 CM)

Press-molded white stoneware; electric
fired, iron sulfate on raised design, bisque
fired, cone 6; glaze fired, cone 04

PHOTOS BY LYNN RENDER

Susan Wink

Nucleus | 2000

DIAMETER: 36 FEET (11 M)

Steel, stone, ceramic, and cement block; drought-tolerant plants

PHOTO BY ARTIST

Nettie Locke Rogers

Junk Yard | 2003

101 X 75 X 15 INCHES (256.5 X 190.5 X 38.1 CM)

Slab-built; glazed; oxidation fired,
cone 5; cast resin, wooden door

PHOTOS BY ARTIST

Will Levi Marshall

Cairt Frieze | 2004

98½ X 236¼ INCHES (250 X 600 CM)

Porcelain; electric fired, cone 10; glazed, cone 10; decals gold/black, cone 018

PHOTOS BY SHANNON TOFT

Dalia Laučkaité-Jakimavičiené
A Window | 2003
23⁹/₁₆ X 55 X ³/₈ INCHES (60 X 140 X 1 CM)
Manufactured tiles, glazes, laser print decals; cone 07, onglaze decals, china paints, gold, and lusters; cone 016
PHOTO BY VIDMANTAS ILLČIUKAS

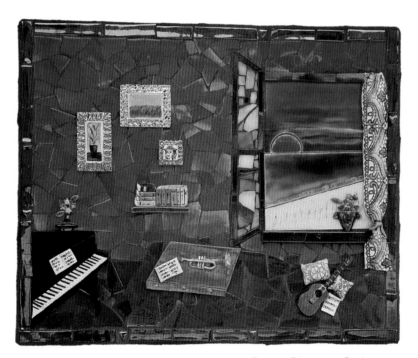

Rose Gispert Quintana
A Piano | 2006

19 X 24 X 1 INCHES (48.3 X 61 X 2.5 CM)

Hand-built and sculpted earthenware;
bisque fired, cone 04; glazed and
underglazed, cone 06; lusters, cone 018

PHOTOS BY BATIA COHEN

Lisa Burt
Nouveau Columbine | 2006
4 X 4 X ¼ INCHES (10.2 X 10.2 X 0.6 CM)
Press-molded stoneware; electric
fired to bisque, cone 04; hand-
painted polychrome, cone 6
PHOTO BY ARTIST

Farrady Newsome

Dark Blue Boxy Wall Tile | 2002

16 X 17 X 6 INCHES (40.6 X 43.2 X 15.2 CM)

Slab-built terra cotta with press-molded attachments; bisque fired, cone 1; brushed glazes, electric fired, cone 05

PHOTO BY ARTIST

Ruth O'Day

Leaf Forms | 2004

EACH: 16 X 36 INCHES (40.6 X 91.4 CM)

Hand-cut sculpture clay; electric fired,
cone 6; embedded in colored stucco

PHOTOS BY ARTIST

Ruth O'Day

Guardian Serpent (detail on facing page) | 2001

WALL: 2 X 125 FEET (0.6 X 38.1 METERS)

Hand-cut sculpture clay; electric fired,
cone 6; colored stucco background

PHOTOS BY ARTIST

Mona M. Shiber

Subtle Energy: Lotus Chakradarshi V | 2004-2005

44 X 17 X 2 INCHES (111.8 X 43.2 X 5.1 CM)

Hand-carved white earthenware slab; stamped with handmade
clay roll stamps; electric fired, cone 03; engobes, oxide
washes; grease pastels drawn over hot tiles

PHOTOS BY M. DEKAY AND ARTIST

Dot Kolentsis
Musician | 2006
11³/₄ X 11³/₄ INCHES (30 X 30 CM)
White earthenware; electric fired, 2102°F
(1100°C), hand-painted maiolica

PHOTO BY JENNI CARTER

Marian Baker

Lobster Time Tile | 2004

6 X 6 X ½ INCHES (15.2 X 15.2 X 1.3 CM)

Press-molded earthenware; electric fired, cone 05,
iron oxide stain rubbed in and wiped off, cone 1

PHOTO BY ARTIST

Jennifer A. Everett
Tile | 2006
3 X 3 X ³/₈ INCHES (7.6 X 7.6 X 1 CM)
Extruded stoneware with stamped
decoration; gas fired in reduction, cone 10
PHOTO BY ARTIST

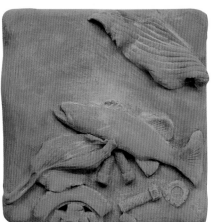

Lois Peterson

Listening at the Edge Series Tile #13 | 2003

13 X 13 X 3 INCHES (33 X 33 X 7.6 CM)

Press-molded stoneware; electric fired,
cone 04; commercial iron finish

PHOTO BY NELL YTSMA

Suzanne Wolfe

Do Women Really Want to Be Men? | 2007

11 3/4 X 11 3/4 X 1/4 INCHES (29.8 X 29.8 X 0.6 CM)

Commercial stoneware; underglaze,
cone 2; laser imagery transfer, cone 01

PHOTO BY BRAD GODA

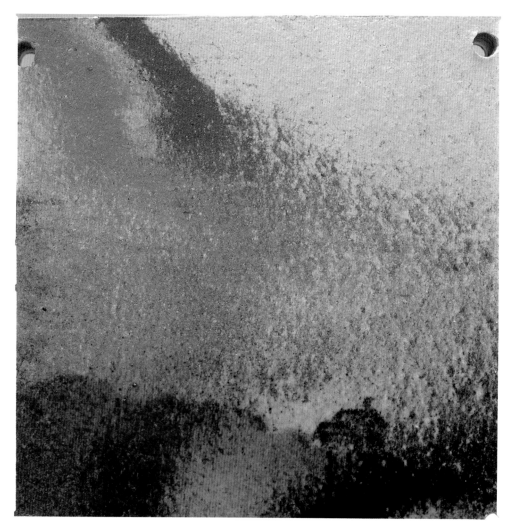

Hwang Jeng-daw

Norwegian Mountain Landscape No. 2 | 2002

3¹⁵/₁₆ X 3¹⁵/₁₆ X ³/₈ INCHES (10 X 10 X 1 CM)

Slab-built porcelain, mixed colored clay; electric fired, cone 9

PHOTO BY ARTIST

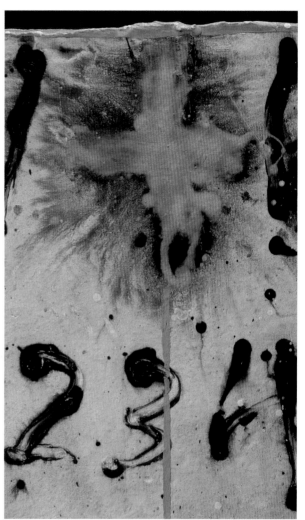

Bede Clarke

Talea | 2004

29 X 29 X 1 INCHES (73.7 X 73.7 X 2.5 CM)

Earthenware; engobes; electric fired, cone 03

PHOTOS BY ARTIST

Lynn H. Felton

Exposed | 2003

12 X 10 X 1 INCHES (30.5 X 25.4 X 2.5 CM)

Hand-built low-fire clay; electric fired,
cone 04; Velvet underglazes, cone 05

PHOTO BY DAVID GULISANO

Garrett Angelich
Sorrowful Bob | 2007
8 X 8 INCHES (20.3 X 20.3 CM)
Press-molded Navajo Wheel stoneware from original
sculpture; terra sigillata, underglaze, nickel oxide
wash and wood shavings; electric fired, cone 04

PHOTO BY ARTIST

Peter A. Davis
Untitled | 2003
4¼ X 8½ INCHES (10.8 X 21.6 CM)
Slip-trailed and painted underglaze;
sgraffitoed with clear glaze, cone 04
PHOTO BY ARTIST

Joan Rothchild Hardin
Dragonflies | 2004
6 X 12 X ¼ INCHES (15.2 X 30.4 X 0.6 CM)
Hand-painted commercial bisque tile;
Amaco glazes; electric fired, cone 05
PHOTO BY JAMES DEE

Sandy Culp
Rainbow Trout | 1997
5 X 6¹/₂ X ¹/₄ INCHES (12.7 X 16.5 X 0.6 CM)
Altered stoneware slab; underglazed,
cone 06; second underglaze layer and
glaze; electric fired in oxidation, cone 6
PHOTO BY BART KASTEN

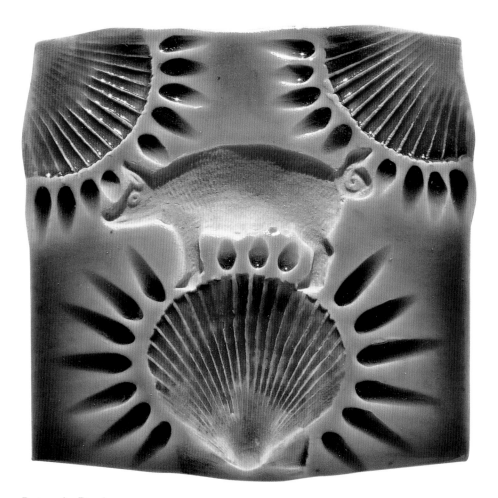

Peter A. Davis
Untitled | 2004

4$\frac{1}{2}$ X 4$\frac{1}{2}$ INCHES (11.4 X 11.4 CM)

Stamped metal, shell, wood; Woody's Turquoise,
Honey Amber, and pink glazes, cone 04

PHOTO BY ARTIST

Elaine Bolz
Toucans | 2002
10 X 12 X ½ INCHES (25.4 X 30.5 X 1.3 CM)
White earthenware clay; electric fired,
cone 02; multi-fired, cone 05; airbrushed
and painted with underglazes
PHOTO BY ARTIST

Dryden Wells

Heavenly Ham | 2006

6 X 4 X ¼ INCHES (15.2 X 10.2 X 0.6 CM)

Hand-rolled porcelain; black oxide wash;
subtractive drawing, reduction fired, cone 6

PHOTO BY WES HARVEY

Lorraine Sutter

Poplar | 2005

13¾ X 5⅞ X ¾ INCHES (35 X 15 X 2 CM)

Slab-built porcelain paper clay

PHOTO BY AK PHOTOS

Keri Huber

Owl, Rabbit, Puffer Fish | 2005
EACH: 2½ X 2½ X ½ INCHES (6.4 X 6.4 X 1.3 CM)
Press-molded earthenware; bisque fired,
cone 04; stain, soda fired, cone 04
PHOTO BY JERRY MATHIASON

Novie Trump

Sea Turtles | 2006

8 X 14 X 1 INCHES (20.3 X 35.6 X 2.5 CM)

Mid-range, outdoor sculpture body clay; electric fired, cone
06; glazed with Mason stains, oxides, and slips, cone 6

PHOTO BY GREG STALEY

Sandy Culp
Pear Pair | 2001
8 X 12 X 1 ½ INCHES (20.3 X 30.5 X 3.8 CM)
Hand-built Lizella clay; bas relief, iron
oxide; electric fired in oxidation, cone 6
PHOTO BY ARTIST

Maggie Mae Beyeler

Ca'd'oro | 2007

6 X 6 X ⁵/₁₆ INCHES (15.2 X 15.2 X 0.8 CM)

Slab-rolled white stoneware; electric fired, cone 6;
laser toner image transfer, cone 04; matte
green/bronze glaze and underglaze stamped text

PHOTO BY MARGOT GEIST

Nan Smith

Katherine | 2004

34 X 22 X 1 1/2 INCHES (86.4 X 55.9 X 3.8 CM)

Tamped and rolled buff earthenware; bisque, electric fired, cone 03; airbrushed and brushed underglaze applied to bisque; glazed, cone 04; color graduated with airbrushed bisque stains

PHOTOS BY ALLEN CHEUVRONT

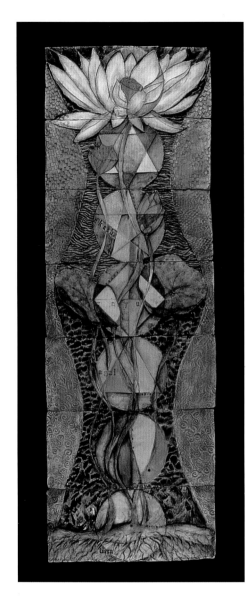

Mona M. Shiber

Sacred Geometry: Lotus Chakradarshi I | 2001

48 X 18 X 2 INCHES (121.9 X 45.7 X 5.1 CM)

Hand-carved stoneware; reduction fired, cone 01
with slips, stain, oxide washes, and glazes

PHOTOS BY M. SHIBER/COMMERCIAL 35; JOSEPH GRUBER (DETAIL)

Stephanie Osser
Dan's French Horn | 2003
10 X 8 X 2 INCHES (25.4 X 20.3 X 2.5 CM)
Press-molded porcelain; reduction
fired, cone 10; underglaze and glaze
PHOTO BY MONICA RIPLEY

Dalia Laučkaité-Jakimavičiené

Angels' Frolics | 2001

29½ X 29½ X 9¹³/₁₆ INCHES (75 X 75 X 25 CM)

Slab-built earthenware; electric fired, cone 07; glazed, cone 05; china paints, gold, silver, platinum lusters, and decals, cone 016; found object

PHOTO BY VIDMANTAS ILLČIUKAS

Linda S. Leighton
Deity | 2005
6 X 7³/₄ X 1¹/₄ INCHES (15.2 X 19.7 X 3.2 CM)
Stoneware; oxidation fired, cone 05;
underglazes, oxide stains, glaze, cone 6;
drawing applied via LazerTran paper
PHOTO BY TERRY TALBOT

Rosalyn Tyge
Dragon Fly Pond | 2005

44 X 21 X 7 INCHES (111.8 X 53.3 X 17.8 CM)

Press-molded and hand-cut white
stoneware tiles; electric fired, cone 6

PHOTO BY DONALD RUTT

Brenda B. Townsend
Dragon Kimono 13 | 2005

23 X 21 INCHES (58.4 X 53.3 CM)

Cut; handmade glazes; raku fired

PHOTO BY CHIP FEISE LOCATION PHOTOGRAPHY

Maggie Mae Beyeler

La Serenissima | 2007

6 X 6 X 2 INCHES (15.2 X 15.2 X 5.1 CM)

Slab-rolled white stoneware; electric fired, cone 6; laser toner image transfer, cone 04; Italian text from Dante stamped with black underglaze

PHOTO BY MARGOT GEIST

Phyllis Pacin

Wisps | 2005

18 X 27 X 1 1/2 INCHES (45.7 X 68.6 X 3.8 CM)

Hand-textured and hand-rolled tile; bisque
fired, cone 05; glazed and raku fired, cone 06

PHOTO BY SIBILA SAVAGE

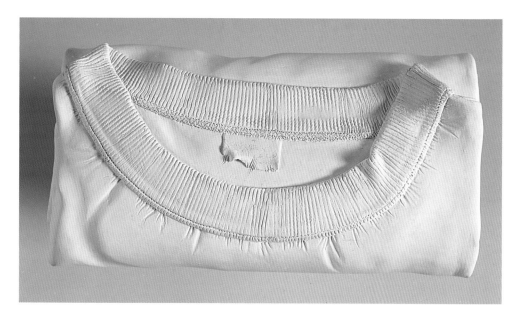

Lorraine Sutter

White T | 2005

4¹¹/₁₆ X 7⁷/₈ X 2⁹/₁₆ INCHES (12 X 20 X 6.5 CM)

Slab- and coil-built low-fire paper
clay; carved and impressed

PHOTO BY AK PHOTOS

Suzanne Wolfe

Boy with Dead Bird | 2007

11³/₄ X 11³/₄ X ¹/₄ INCHES (29.8 X 29.8 X 0.6 CM)

Commercial stoneware; underglaze, cone 2;
laser imagery transfer, cone 01; glaze,
cone 05; china paint, cone 017

PHOTO BY BRAD GODA

Mary-Paige Cannon
By My Side | 2007
3⁷/₈ X 4¹/₂ X ³/₈ INCHES (9.8 X 11.5 X 1 CM)
White stoneware with underglaze;
electric fired, cone 6
PHOTO BY ANNA V. FREEMAN

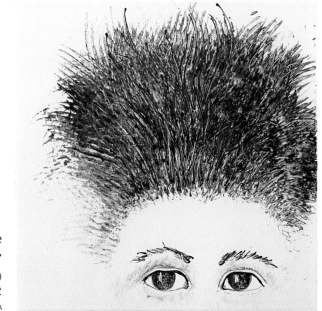

Suzanne Wolfe
Girl with Wild Hair | 2007
11³/₄ X 11³/₄ X ¹/₄ INCHES (29.8 X 29.8 X 0.6 CM)
Commercial stoneware; underglaze, cone 2
PHOTO BY BRAD GODA

Kathleen Koltes
Ione | 2007
6 X 6 X ³⁄₈ INCHES (15.2 X 15.2 X 1 CM)
Slab-rolled stoneware; silkscreened,
hand-carved eye stamp; underglazes; electric glaze-fired, cone 6
PHOTO BY MARGOT GEIST

Kimberly Rorick

Orange House Tile | 2006

5¹/₂ X 3³/₄ INCHES (14 X 9.5 CM)

Slab-rolled porcelain; underglazed;
electric fired, cone 6

PHOTO BY ACCU COLOR

Nawal Motawi
Karim Motawi

4x8 Sunflower, Retro Lime | 2006

8 X 4 X ⁵/₈ INCHES (20.3 X 10.2 X 1.6 CM)

Press-molded stoneware; electric
fired, cone 04; glazed, cone 6

PHOTO BY JERRY ANTHONY

Melody Dalessandro Bonnema

Remembering Tom Thomson II | 2004
7 X 7 X ½ INCHES (17.8 X 17.8 X 1.3 CM)
Hand-rolled stoneware; gas fired in reduction, cone 9
PHOTO BY STEVE TRAFICONTE

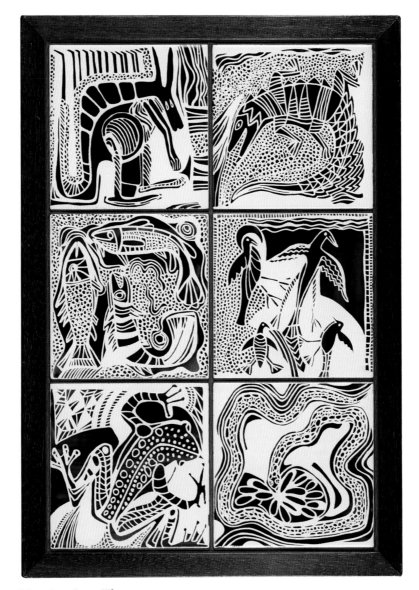

Harriet Ann Thompson

Australian Animals | 2003

14 1/2 X 10 1/4 X 3/4 INCHES (36.8 X 26 X 1.9 CM)

White tiles, glaze, cone 06; Australian
Aboriginal-style markings

PHOTO BY D. KENT THOMPSON

Peter Wareing

Figure in the Forest | 1995

23⁹/₁₆ X 29⁷/₁₆ INCHES (60 X 75 CM)

Commercial bisque tile; tube lined, coloured glazes, overlaid with transparent glaze; cone 1

PHOTO BY ARTIST

Tim Ludwig

Agen Tulip | 2006

12 X 9 X 2½ INCHES (30.5 X 22.9 X 6.4 CM)

Red earthenware with slips
and Mason stains; cone 06

PHOTO BY RANDY SMITH

Nawal Motawi
Karim Motawi

4x4 Lotus, Green Oak | 2007

4 X 4 X 5/8 INCHES (10.2 X 10.2 X 1.6 CM)

Press-molded stoneware; electric
fired, cone 04; glazed, cone 6

PHOTO BY JERRY ANTHONY

Laura A. Reutter

Reverie | 2006

17 X 12 X ½ INCH (43.2 X 30.5 X 1.3 CM)

Press-molded stoneware, grout; electric fired, bisqued, cone 05; glazed, cone 5

PHOTO BY FRANK ROSS

Brenda Bennett (Lyon)
Dragonfly | 2006
4⁵/₁₆ X 4⁵/₁₆ X ³/₁₆ INCHES (11 X 11 X 0.5 CM)
Hand-carved stoneware; electric fired, cone 8
PHOTO BY GARY WEX

Norma Hanlon
Kirsten Walstead
Spring Morning Tile Mural | 2005
48 X 24 X 2 INCHES (121.9 X 61 X 5.1 CM)
Press-molded stoneware; electric fired, cone 4
PHOTO BY DIGIGRAPHICS

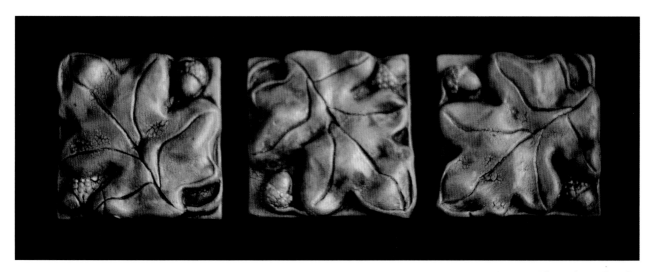

Nancy Chevalier Guido
Oak Leaf Tiles | 2002
EACH: 4 X 4 X 1 INCHES (10.2 X 10.2 X 2.5 CM)
Press-molded terra cotta; multi-fired in electric
kiln, cone 6; layered stains and engobes
PHOTO BY BRIAN GUIDO

Sheri Ukrainetz
Blue Mosaic Tile | 2007
4¹/₂ X 4¹/₂ X ¹/₄ INCHES (11.4 X 11.4 X 0.6 CM)
Slab stoneware; incised and stamped;
electric fired, cone 5, commercial glaze
PHOTO BY BILL HARASYMCHUK

Bede Clarke

Vesuvius | 2004

12 X 12 X 1 INCHES (30.5 X 30.5 X 2.5 CM)

Earthenware; engobes; electric fired, cone 03

PHOTO BY ARTIST

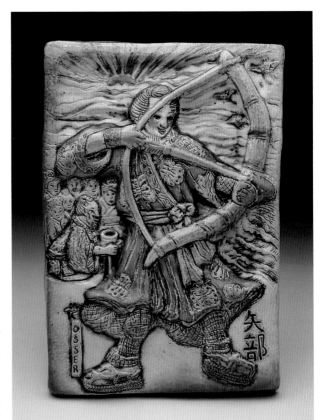

Stephanie Osser

Potter/Archer | 2006

8¼ X 5½ X 1¼ INCHES (21 X 14 X 3.2 CM)

Press-molded porcelain; soda fired,
cone 10; underglaze and glaze

PHOTO BY MONICA RIPLEY

Ji Youl Choi
Spring | 2006
EACH: 5 7/8 X 5 7/8 X 3/16 INCHES (15 X 15 X 0.5 CM)
Porcelain; electric fired, cone 10
PHOTO BY ARTIST

Marta Matray

Three Silly Tiles | 2005

TALLEST: 4 X 3 X ½ INCHES (10.2 X 7.6 X 1.3 CM)

Hand-built porcelain; soda glaze, cone 10

PHOTO BY PETER LEE

Tony Moore

Botanicals and Cross | 2006

11 X 11 X ½ INCHES (27.9 X 27.9 X 1.3 CM)

Wood-fired stoneware; impressed
botanicals, slip; multi-fired, cone 10

PHOTO BY HOWARD GOODMAN

Hanna Lore Hombordy
Autumn Rain | 2006
11 X 21 X ¾ INCHES (27.9 X 53.3 X 1.9 CM)
Earthenware; electric fired; hand-
painted and airbrushed underglazes
PHOTO BY ARTIST

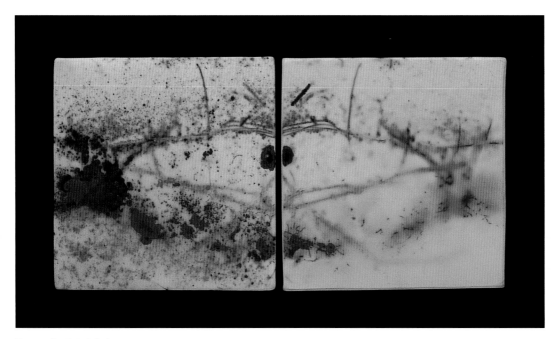

Brenda McMahon

Metamorphosis. Fire Painting | 2006

4 X 8 X ¼ INCHES (10.2 X 20.3 X 0.6 CM)

Slab-rolled stoneware; saggar fired, cone 04

PHOTO BY JASON LACHTARA

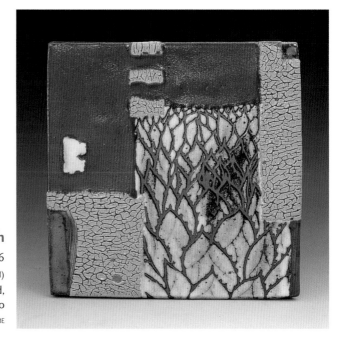

Jeff Reich

Agave with Red | 2006

9 X 9 X ¼ INCHES (22.9 X 22.9 X 0.6 CM)

Hand-built stoneware; reduction fired,
cone 10; crawling glaze and glaze sgraffito

PHOTO BY FARRADAY NEWSOME

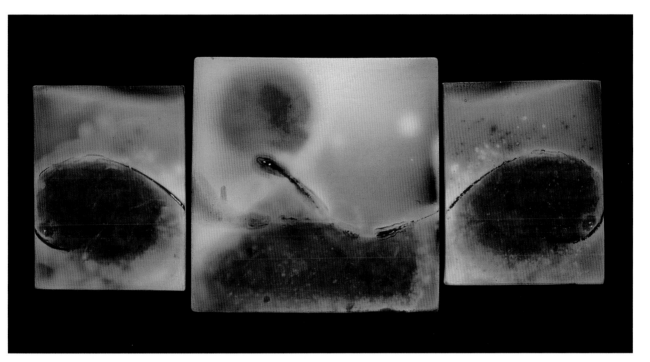

Brenda McMahon
Planetary Moonrise. Fire Painting | 2006
5 X 15 X ¼ INCHES (12.7 X 38.1 X 0.6 CM)
Slab-rolled stoneware; saggar fired, cone 04
PHOTO BY JASON LACHTARA

Carrie Anne Parks

Birds and Berries Tiles (detail on facing page) | 2002

15 1/8 X 21 1/4 X 2 INCHES (38.4 X 54 X 5.1 CM)

Press-molded earthenware; electric fired,
cone 06; underglazed, cone 05

PHOTOS BY ARTIST

Daniel Gegen

Accountable? | 1999

6 X 18 X ¾ INCHES (15.2 X 45.7 X 1.9 CM)

Terra cotta; electric fired, cone 03; black copper oxide wash and terra sigillata

PHOTO BY ARTIST

Deb Mary LeAir

Abstract Landscape | 2006

10 X 30 X 1 INCHES (25.4 X 76.2 X 2.5 CM)

Hand-carved earthenware with terra sigillata surface; electric fired, cone 04; copper wash, cone 05

PHOTO BY LARRY SANDERS

Marcia Hovland
Polly's World | 2006
10 X 5 X ¾ INCHES (25.4 X 12.7 X 1.9 CM)
Low relief; cone 05, hand painted
PHOTO BY ARTIST

Kurt Brian Webb

*Dance of Death Orchestra Pit
(Ceramic Toy Theatre Facade)* | 2006

10 X 9 X 1 INCHES (25.4 X 22.9 X 2.5 CM)

Carved stoneware; woodfired with soda

PHOTO BY ARTIST

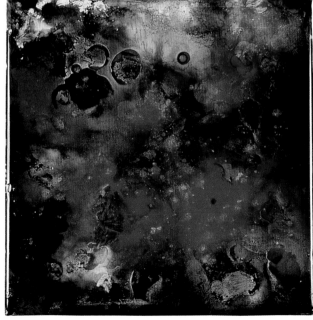

Cynthia Luhrs

Color Series #1 | 2006

6 X 6 INCHES (15.2 X 15.2 CM)

Ceramic; painted with acrylics, inks, and
Pearl Ex powders; glazed; clear resin

PHOTO BY LYNN RUCK

John Wehrle
Trout and Tools | 2002
48 X 60 INCHES (121.9 X 152.4 CM)
Commercial 12-inch (30.5 cm) terra-cotta
pavers; glazed, electric fired, cone 04
PHOTO BY ARTIST

Richard Notkin

The Sleep of Reason (after Goya) | 2006

4 1/4 X 20 X 1 3/4 INCHES (10.8 X 50.8 X 4.4 CM)

Press-molded terra cotta; electric fired, cone 5; unglazed

PHOTOS BY ARTIST

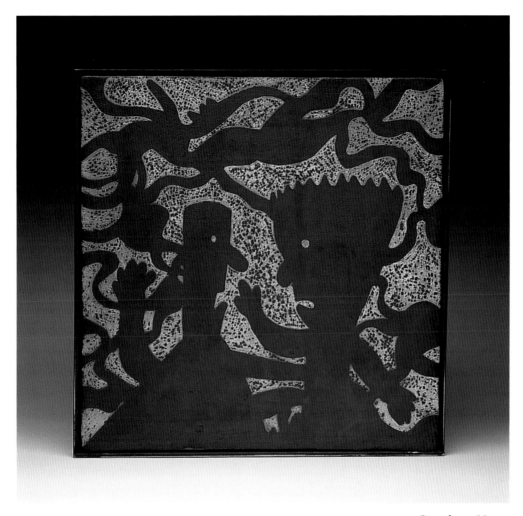

Stephen Horn

Haniwa Couple | 2005

16 X 16 X 1 ½ INCHES (40.6 X 40.6 X 3.8 CM)

Hand-built stoneware; gas fired,
cone 5; glaze, cone 5; steel frame

PHOTO BY SCOTT BRINEGAR

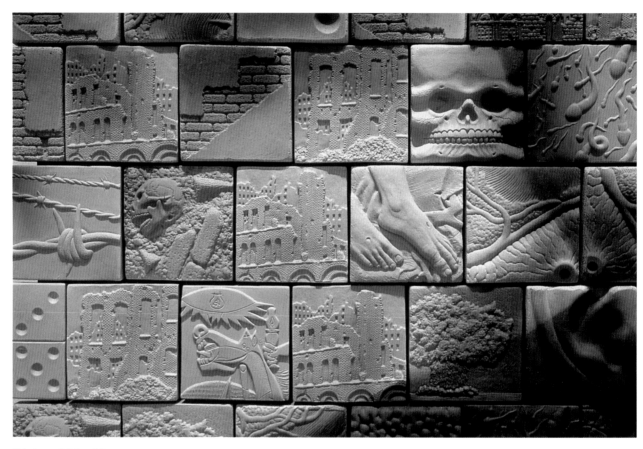

Richard Notkin

All Nations Have Their Moment of Foolishness | 2007

46 X 60¼ X 4½ INCHES (116.8 X 153 X 11.4 CM)

Press-molded earthenware; gasfired in sawdust-filled saggars, cone 04; unglazed; post-fired watercolor highlights

PHOTO BY ARTIST

Joan Rasmussen
One of Many | 2006
EACH: 6 X 6 X 2½ INCHES (15.2 X 15.2 X 6.4 CM)
Hand-built, terra cotta clay; underglazes,
low-fire glazes, and stains
PHOTO BY DAVID GULISANO

Deb Mary LeAir

My Burma Road | 2006

24 X 24 X 1 INCHES (61 X 61 X 2.5 CM)

Hand-carved earthenware, terra sigilatta
surface; electric fired, cone 04; glaze
and copper wash, cone 05

PHOTO BY LARRY SANDERS

Mary Philpott

Birds in Wisteria Art Nouveau Tile in Quarter-Sawn Oak Frame | 2006

TILE: 12 X 6 INCHES (30.5 X 15.2 CM)

Hand-carved, -pressed, and glazed porcelain; electric fired, multi-fired, cone 7

PHOTO BY ARTIST

Scott J. Ziegler

The Deafening Sounds of Reality | 2007

8½ X 5 X 1½ INCHES (21.6 X 12.7 X 3.8 CM)

Slip-cast porcelain; electric fired, cone 6; slips and glazes

PHOTO BY JEFFREY DIONESOTES

Peter A. Davis

Untitled | 2003

8$^{1}/_{2}$ X 8$^{1}/_{2}$ INCHES (21.6 X 21.6 CM)

Molded and stamped white clay; Woody's
Turquoise, green wash, Honey Amber, and
purple slip, cone 04

PHOTO BY ARTIST

Jonathan Nicklow

Let Her Bee | 2006

8 X 8 X ¾ INCHES (20.3 X 20.3 X 1.9 CM)

Low-fire white clay; electric fired, cone
04; slab-rolled, relief sculpture, stamped
elements, oil paint, tar and varnish

PHOTO BY ARTIST

Jeff Reich

Agave | 2006

9 X 9 X ¼ INCHES (22.9 X 22.9 X 0.6 CM)

Hand-built stoneware; reduction fired, cone 10;
crawling glaze and glaze sgraffito

PHOTO BY FARRADAY NEWSOME

Linda Kliewer
Sprekelia Flower | 2006
10 X 10 INCHES (25.4 X 25.4 CM)
Stoneware; electric fired, cone 5
PHOTO BY COURTNEY FRISSE

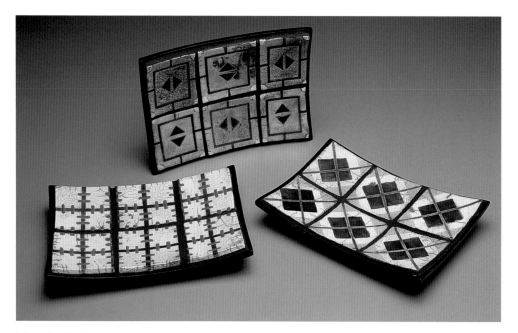

Marcia Reiver

Rhythm in Three | 2006

EACH: 7³/4 X 11 X 1 INCHES (19.7 X 27.9 X 2.5 CM)

Slab-rolled and hand-cut;
raku fired; black bamboo tray

PHOTO BY JOHN CARLANO

Rena Fafalios

Untitled | 2007

3¹/4 X 3¹/4 X ¹/4 INCHES (8.3 X 8.3 X 0.6 CM)

Stoneware; bisque fired,
cone 06, metallic waxes

PHOTO BY JAMES DEE

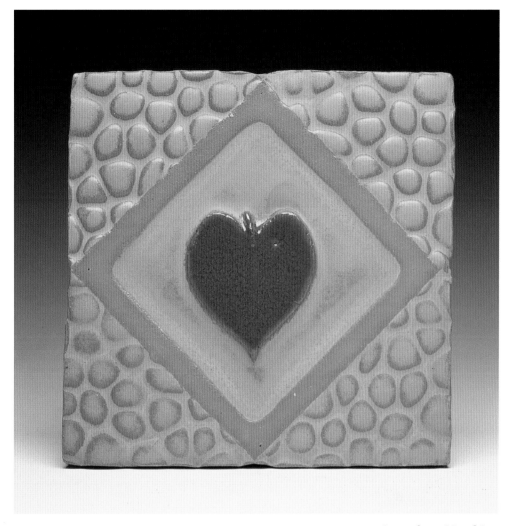

Jonathan Hawkins

On the Pathway to the Heart of My Garden | 2006

6 X 6 X ¹¹⁄₁₆ INCHES (15.2 X 15.2 X 1.7 CM)

Pressed and carved earthenware; electric
fired, cone 03; glazed, cone 05

PHOTO BY JASON LACHTARA

Dot Kolentsis

Persian Motif | 2006

3 15/16 X 3 15/16 INCHES (10 X 10 CM)

Press-molded white earthenware;
fired, 2192°F (1200°C); glazed

PHOTO BY JENNI CARTER

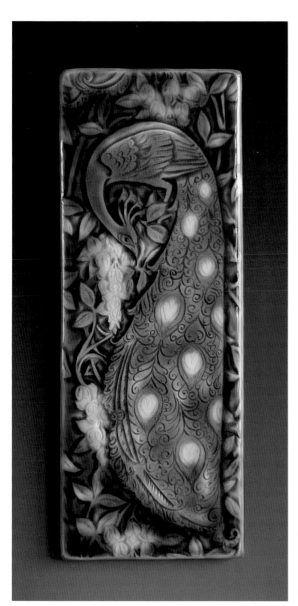

Connie Pike

Leaves | 2005

5¼ X 3¾ INCHES (13.3 X 9.5 CM)

Stoneware pressed from plaster
mold; gas fired, cone 10

PHOTO BY ARTIST

Mary Philpott

Art Nouveau Peacock Art Tile | 2006

16 X 6 INCHES (40.6 X 15.2 CM)

Hand-carved, -pressed, and glazed porcelain; electric fired, multi-fired, cone 7

PHOTO BY ARTIST

Michael P. Skiersch

Water's Edge | 2005

18 X 30 X ¾ INCHES (45.7 X 56.5 X 1.9 CM)

Press-molded stoneware; electric fired, cone 05; glazed, cone 6

PHOTO BY GUY NICOL

Dave Lynas
Old Barn | 2006
5 1/4 X 11 1/4 X 5/8 INCHES (13.3 X 28.6 X 1.6 CM)
Roulette-impressed porcelain;
gas fired in reduction, cone 9
PHOTO BY JEFF FREY & ASSOCIATES

Merla Frazey-Jordan

Dog Smile | 2006

11 X 15 X 1 INCHES (27.9 X 38.1 X 2.5 CM)

High-relief stoneware; electric
fired, cone 05; watercolor

PHOTO BY ARTIST

Caryn van Wagtendonk
Stan's Mittens | 2006
10 X 5 X ³⁄₈ INCHES (25.4 X 12.7 X 1 CM)
Terra cotta; low-fire colored slips
with sgraffito drawing, black stain
wash; glazed, cone 04, electric fired
PHOTO BY ARTIST

Daniel Gegen

Coffee on Deck | 2001

6 X 6 X ¾ INCHES (15.2 X 15.2 X 1.9 CM)

Terra cotta; electric fired, cone 03; black copper oxide wash and terra sigillata

PHOTO BY ARTIST

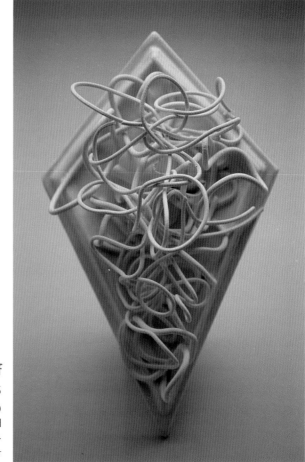

Danielle Booroff

Ornamental Space I | 2006

8¼ X 5⅛ X 2⅜ INCHES (21 X 13 X 6 CM)

Press-molded earthenware with extruded details; electric fired, cone 04; glazed, cone 04

PHOTO BY ARTIST

Sarah Raymond
We'll All Have Tea | 2007

5⁷/₈ X 15³/₄ X 1³/₁₆ INCHES (15 X 40 X 3 CM)

Hand-built stoneware; double-walled construction; underglaze painted with sgraffito drawing; electric fired, cone 6

PHOTO BY VINCE NOGUCHI

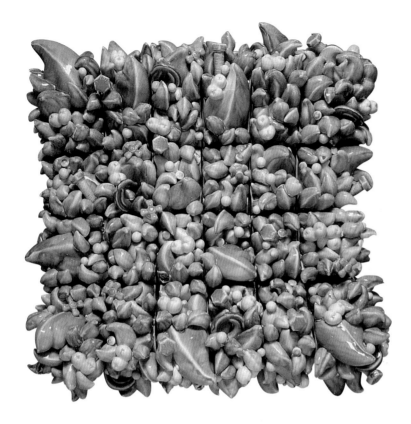

Susan Beiner

Perpetual Recollection | 2004

45 X 52 X 8 INCHES (114.3 X 132.1 X 20.3 CM)

Slip-cast and assembled
porcelain; gas fired, cone 6

PHOTOS BY SUSAN EINSTEIN

Melita Greenleaf
Discarded | 2004
8 X 8 X 3 INCHES (20.3 X 20.3 X 7.6 CM)
Hand-built, self-glazing black
clay; electric fired, cone 6
PHOTO BY ARTIST

Judith Berk King

One Slice Left… | 2006

6 X 10 X 1 INCHES (15.2 X 25.4 X 2.5 CM)

Earthenware; electric fired,
cone 04; glazed, cone 06

PHOTO BY ARTIST

Merla Frazey-Jordan

Grandma's Phone Call | 2006

12 X 12 X 1 INCHES (30.5 X 30.5 X 2.5 CM)

High-relief stoneware; electric
fired, cone 05; watercolor

PHOTO BY ARTIST

Craig Wood

Bob & Carolyn in the '60s | 2007

11 ⁷/₈ X 8³/₄ X ¹/₄ INCHES (30.1 X 30.1 X 22.2 CM)

Slab-built stoneware; bisque fired, cone 04; black
wax resist; handmade glazes; oxidation fired, cone 6

PHOTO BY DON WHEELER

Tony Moore
Botanicals and Cross | 2006
11 X 11 X ½ INCHES (27.9 X 27.9 X 1.3 CM)
Wood-fired stoneware; impressed
botanicals, slip; multi-fired, cone 10
PHOTO BY HOWARD GOODMAN

Brenda McMahon
Eternal Cosmos. Fire Painting | 2006
7 X 7 X ¼ INCHES (17.8 X 17.8 X 0.6 CM)
Slab-rolled stoneware; saggar fired, cone 04
PHOTO BY JASON LACHTARA

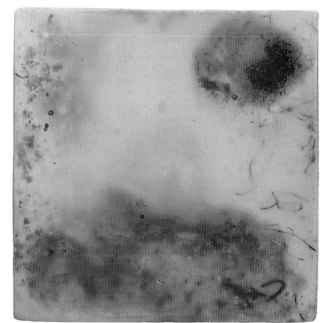

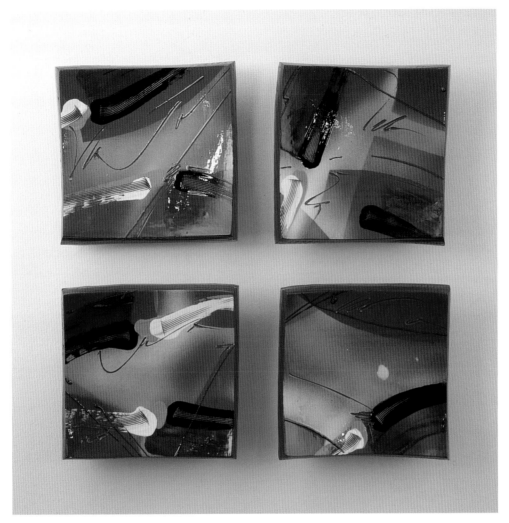

Michael Lemke
Earthenware Wall Tiles | 2006
EACH: 8 X 8 X 2 INCHES (20.3 X 20.3 X 5.1 CM)
Slump-molded earthenware; electric
firings with slips; clear glaze, cone 04
PHOTO BY ARTIST

Tim Ludwig

Crown Imperial | 2006

11 X 9 X 2 INCHES (27.9 X 22.9 X 5.1 CM)

Red earthenware with slips
and Mason stains; cone 06

PHOTO BY RANDY SMITH

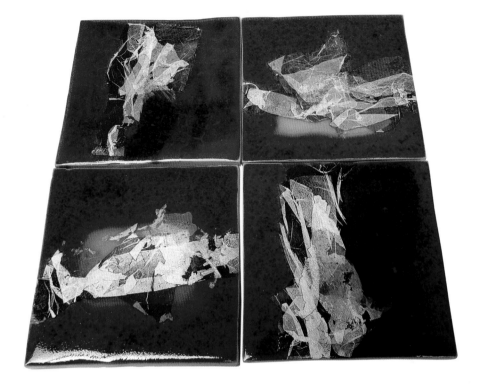

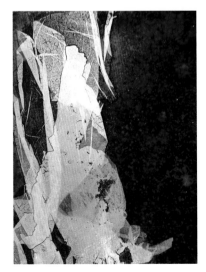

Greg Daly

Decorated Tiles with Gold and Silver Leaf | 2006

EACH: 5⅞ X 5⅞ X ⁵⁄₁₆ INCHES (15 X 15 X 0.8 CM)

Cut stoneware; glaze-on-glaze gas fired, reduction fired cone 9; gold and silver leaf; electric fired, cone 017

PHOTOS BY ARTIST

Acknowledgments

Beautiful handmade tiles are everywhere in the world, yet tile artists often don't get the kind of formal artistic recognition that other ceramists do. They deserve a 500 book all their own, as well as a huge heap of gratitude from us here at Lark for their contributions.

But this marvelous collection exists also because of the commitment of a tireless editorial and production team: Shannon Quinn-Tucker kept the whole train running on time; Dawn Dillingham picked up where others had left off and never missed a beat; Shannon Yokeley and Jeff Hamilton did the thankless digital work; and Matt Shay took particular delight in doing the creative layout work. Great work, and humble thanks to all.

—Suzanne J. E. Tourtillott

About the Juror

Angelica Pozo, a studio artist living and working in Cleveland, Ohio, has been an instructor at several schools, including The Cleveland Institute of Art and the School of Visual Arts at Pennsylvania State University. Ms. Pozo's resume includes numerous workshop and artist residencies; her work has received several awards and is featured in several permanent collections, including the American Craft Museum, New York; and her writing and art were featured in *The Penland Book of Ceramics: Master Classes in Ceramic Techniques* (Lark, 2003), and she is also the author of *Making & Installing Handmade Tiles* (Lark, 2005).

Index to the Contributors